PREGN
FROM CON
TO BIRTH

June Thompson

Consultant Editor
Gila Leiter, M.D.

MARSHALL PUBLISHING • LONDON

A Marshall Edition
Conceived, edited and designed by
Marshall Editions
170 Piccadilly, London W1V 9DD

First published in the UK in 1998 by
Marshall Publishing Ltd

Copyright © 1998 Marshall Editions
Developments Ltd

ISBN: 1-84028-039-5

Originated in the UK by DP Graphics, Trowbridge
Printed in China by Excel Printing

Project Editor Esther Labi
Designer Philip Letsu
Picture Editor Zilda Tandy
DTP Editor Lesley Gilbert
Managing Editor Lindsay McTeague
Production Editor Rebecca Clunes
Editorial Director Sophie Collins
Art Director Sean Keogh
Production Nikki Ingram

Consultant Editor

Gila Leiter, M.D.
Dr. Leiter is Assistant Clinical Professor, Mount
Sinai School of Medicine, New York, and has a
private practice in Park Avenue, New York. She is
a fellow of the American College of Obstetrics and
Gynecology and a certified member of the
American Board of Obstetrics and Gynecology. She
has four children.

Note

Note: The terms "he" and "she", used in
alternate sections, refer to people of both sexes,
unless a topic or sequence of photographs applies
only to a male or female.

INDEX

See also technical terms on p. 83

USING THIS BOOK

This guide is divided into six subject areas: 1 Conception; 2 Health and Diet; 3 Exercise and Relaxation; 4 Antenatal Care, Labour, and Birth; 5 You and Your Baby; 6 Your Personal File. If you know which subject area you wish to access, turn to the relevant tab. On each tab you will find a detailed table of the contents of that section of the guide. If you are unsure where to find the information you need, turn to the alphabetical index on page 3.

Subject heading
Each double-page spread is self contained, to give a concise treatment of a subject's major points of interest.

Introduction
Running text gives a brief overview of the subject under discussion, highlighting important factors, common problems, and easy solutions.

Tab
Colour-coded subject dividers enable you to turn quickly and easily to the section you need. Each divider offers a contents listing of the subjects included on pages that bear the same coloured band.

Boxed information
Subjects of related interest and quick-reference charts appear in coloured boxes, enhancing reference value and making the text more user-friendly.

Numbered points
Easy-to-follow sequences of step-by-step words and photographs explain all aspects of pregnancy.

Colour photographs
A combination of practical and inspirational photographs and illustrations complement the informative text.

Conception

CONCEPTION

Deciding to have a baby is one of the most important decisions you and your partner will make. Healthy parents are more likely to have healthy babies, so the healthier you are before you conceive and during pregnancy, the better it will be for you and your baby.

Pregnancy and childbirth have never been safer in the developed world than they are today, but ensuring you are in good shape will make it easier for you to cope with pregnancy, the delivery and the demands of a new baby.

Preparing for pregnancy should begin at least three months before you start trying to conceive. To help you prepare, this section looks at the variety of steps you should take to plan your pregnancy and the questions you may need to ask.

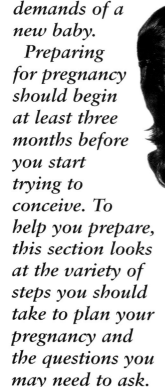

PLANNING AHEAD

By planning your preconceptual programme, you and your spouse can ensure you are in the best of health and are aware of any potential hazards or hereditary factors that could affect your health and that of your baby. There are a number of steps you and your partner should take at least three months before trying to conceive.

REVIEW YOUR LIFESTYLE AND GENERAL HEALTH

■ Do you smoke cigarettes, drink alcohol or use drugs such as marijuana, cocaine or heroin? If so, you can seriously harm yourself and your baby. See pp. 10–11 for advice on changing your habits.

■ Are you reasonably fit? If not, see pp. 44–47 for improving your fitness.

■ What is your general health and immunization status? For advice on health and immunization checks see pp. 8–9. Discuss any problems with your doctor.

REVIEW YOUR NUTRITION

■ Are you overweight or underweight? Being significantly over- or underweight may reduce your chances of conceiving (see p. 11).

■ Do you eat fewer than three meals a day, or constantly snack? Do you eat a special diet? Eating a balanced diet is essential for a healthy baby. See pp. 28–29 for advice about nutrition.

STOP USING CONTRACEPTION

■ If you use an intrauterine device (IUD) have it removed before you plan to become pregnant, since it can increase the risk of an infection.

■ Stop using the contraceptive pill at least two menstrual cycles before trying to conceive. It may take a few months for "natural" periods to resume, and there is also evidence that the pill can affect the absorption of certain vitamins and minerals.

■ In the meantime, use natural family-planning methods or a barrier method in the fertile period.

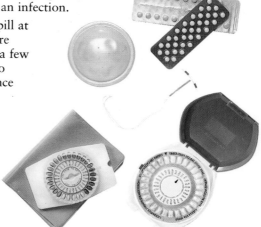

ARE YOU AT RISK FROM ANIMALS OR FOOD

■ Do you have a cat or live on a farm? Do you eat unpasteurized or mould-ripened cheeses or drink unpasteurized milk? You could contract an infection from food or animals that could harm your baby. See pp. 24–25 for advice on how to help avoid the danger.

HAZARDS IN YOUR HOME AND AT WORK

Before you conceive, check your exposure to pollutants, which can affect your unborn baby or may lead to a miscarriage.

Health hazards at work

Try to find out about hazards at work such as chemicals, gases, or radiation from x-ray equipment. Recent studies about the harmful effects on the foetus of visual display units (VDU) have found no evidence of any risk, but you may wish to reduce your daily exposure. Talk to your employer or health and safety officer if you have any concerns about your safety at work. (See also pp. 44–47 for further advice on safeguarding your health at work when pregnant.)

Chemicals to avoid

Mercury may be found in tuna fish, agricultural chemicals, weedkillers and dental amalgam fillings. Avoid eating too much tuna, handling weedkillers or insecticides for pest control, and using cleaning products that may be toxic.

Lead can be found in:

■ Drinking water: If you live in a house with old pipes, ask your local water board to test your drinking water. In the meantime, filter your water.

■ Old flaking paint: You may wish to have this tested by a professional lead inspector. If you decide to remove old paint, have it done professionally and stay away from the area while the work is going on. If you remove the paint yourself, wear protective clothing and cover your face and hair.

■ Petrol: Use lead-free petrol, and, if you live near a main road, use net curtains.

RESPONSIBLE FATHERHOOD

Giving your baby a good start in life is dependent on your own health as well as that of your partner's. You produce sperm all the time but they require 100 days to mature fully and the quantity and quality of the sperm can be affected by:

■ Excessive alcohol and smoking

■ Drugs

■ Poor nutrition

■ Obesity

■ Stress

■ Environmental pollution, including exposure to chemicals and toxins.

PRECONCEPTION CHECKS

Before you conceive, your doctor can make a variety of health checks. These include taking your full medical and obstetric history, establishing whether you have had childhood diseases such as chickenpox or any sexually transmitted diseases, and checking your immunity to rubella (German measles). You should be offered advice about any persistent or permanent medical problems you may have, such as high blood pressure or diabetes, as some conditions require special attention during pregnancy. Your doctor will talk to you about genetic testing, should you require it, and it is also essential that you check with him or her about any prescribed or non-prescription medications you take, to make sure they will be safe for you and your baby while you are pregnant.

CHECK ANY MEDICAL CONDITIONS

Do you have or have you ever had:

■ A medical condition such as asthma, diabetes, high blood pressure, epilepsy or a family history of these?

■ A history of miscarriages?

■ A sexually transmitted disease such as herpes, chlamydia or a venereal disease?

Many women with medical conditions have a straightforward pregnancy. Sometimes, however, problems can arise, and special precautions may be necessary. To reduce the risk of complications you should review your full medical history with your doctor before you become pregnant. Precautions or treatment can then be recommended if necessary. Do not stop taking any medicines unless advised by your doctor.

CHECK YOUR IMMUNIZATION STATUS

■ Have you been immunized against infectious diseases such as rubella (German measles) or measles?

■ Do you plan to travel to a foreign country when pregnant?

Although childhood infectious diseases are rare during pregnancy, if you catch rubella in early pregnancy, or chickenpox around the time of birth, your baby may suffer serious complications. Your immunity can be tested by a simple blood test. If necessary, you can be immunized against rubella but you will be advised to wait three months after the vaccination before conceiving. Many doctors also advise updating immunizations for other diseases such as mumps, hepatitis B and tetanus.

If you plan to travel or live in a foreign country while pregnant, certain other immunizations such as yellow fever or typhoid may be recommended. Because some shots cannot be given to pregnant women, or take time to administer, check with your doctor and plan ahead if you are going to need them.

REVIEW YOUR FAMILY HISTORY

Although it is not possible to cure many birth defects, or even to prevent them happening (some of the most common are still chance events), breakthroughs have been made in identifying those people at risk of having a child with an abnormality and of screening them for those abnormalities. In some cases, two parents carrying the gene for a disorder are needed; in others, only one affected parent can pass the trait on to their baby. If there is anyone who suffers from one of the conditions listed below in either of your close families (parents, brothers and sisters or first cousins), it is worth seeking help before you try to conceive:

■ Genetic disorders such as cystic fibrosis, sickle cell anaemia or trait, thalassemia or Tay-Sachs disease.

■ Birth defects such as Down's syndrome, Turner syndrome, congenital heart defects, cleft palate or hare lip.

Genetic screening or counselling involves taking you and your partner's complete medical history, and then eliminating the possibilities of your passing a trait on to your baby. If it is discovered that the odds of your baby being affected by a serious defect are higher than you consider acceptable, you may be able to consider in vitro fertilization (IVF) using donated eggs or sperm, or adoption.

SCREENING TESTS FOR GENETIC DISORDERS

■ Screening of genetic disorders such as those mentioned above can be carried out with special blood tests on both partners. If both are found to be carriers, each child will have a one in four chance of being affected with the disease.

■ Some disorders are linked mainly to specific ethnic groups. For instance, sickle cell disease occurs more frequently among people of African or Caribbean origin; thalassemia among those of Mediterranean and Southeast Asian descent and Tay-Sachs disease among Ashkenazi Jews.

■ If you are a carrier of the sickle cell or thalassemia trait, you will not have the condition and its presence will not affect you during your pregnancy.

Other tests

Other tests you might like to consider include a test for rhesus positive or negative blood (see pp. 64–65) and for immunity to toxoplasmosis, which may occur if your diet includes undercooked meat (see pp. 24–25).

DENTAL CHECKS

Although you should continue to visit your dentist during pregnancy, have a dental check before you conceive. This will help ensure that your teeth and gums are healthy during pregnancy and avoid the need for any X-rays while you are pregnant. You may also wish to have any mercury fillings changed. Don't forget to remind the dentist of your condition if you visit while you are pregnant.

CHANGING YOUR HABITS

Being under- or overweight, smoking and excessive alcohol and drug intake can reduce your chances of conceiving. Both partners should take steps to change their habits before you try to become pregnant.

WHY STOP SMOKING OR TAKING DRUGS?

There is lots of evidence to show that smoking is harmful to your baby before, during, and after birth, as it lowers the amount of oxygen and nourishment the baby receives. The risks of smoking on your baby's health include:

■ Low birthweight

■ Increased likelihood of miscarriage or stillbirth

■ Increased likelihood of cot death

■ Increased likelihood of respiratory infections, asthma and ear infections

■ Likelihood of being shorter than children of non-smoking parents.

Nicotine patches and nicotine gum can be helpful in stopping smoking, but are not recommended for use in pregnancy.

Taking drugs such as cocaine or heroin during pregnancy puts your baby at risk of miscarriage, premature or stillbirth, or it may be born addicted to the drug. To be weaned off drugs, ask your doctor to refer you for specialist help.

ALCOHOL

Alcohol in your bloodstream can cross the placenta and enter your baby's bloodstream. Heavy drinking can lead to a miscarriage in the early stages of pregnancy or have a damaging effect on your baby's health. Babies of heavy drinkers may be born with a range of physical and mental problems known as fetal alcohol syndrome.

Babies with this syndrome are shorter and lighter in weight than normal babies, have small heads, abnormal features and are usually mentally handicapped. They may also be hyperactive and have severe behaviour problems.

■ The amount you drink can reduce your fertility and ability to conceive.

■ The safest approach is to stop drinking altogether while you try to conceive and when you are pregnant. Otherwise, reduce your alcohol consumption to not more than one or two units (see below) once or twice a week.

■ Getting drunk or binge drinking is particularly dangerous.

One unit of alcohol equals half a pint of beer, a glass of wine or a single measure of spirits.

INCREASE YOUR FOLIC ACID INTAKE

■ Scientific studies have found that increasing your levels of folic acid in the 12 weeks before and after conception can significantly reduce the risk of your baby being born with spina bifida, a cleft palate and hare lip.

■ Folic acid is one of the B vitamins. Good sources include green leafy vegetables; wholewheat bread and fortified cereals; oranges and bananas; milk, yoghurt and cheese; beans and pulses such as black-eyed beans and lentils; yeast or malt extracts.

■ It is generally recommended that you take a supplement of 400 micrograms (0.4 mg) of folic acid daily in tablet form from before you try to conceive and for the first 12 weeks of pregnancy.

CHECK YOUR WEIGHT

Being significantly under- or overweight may reduce your chances of conceiving and the health of your baby is also influenced by your weight.

■ If you are underweight because you are not eating enough, you could be low in vital nutrients such as vitamins, iron and calcium, which can affect both your own and your baby's health.

■ If you are so underweight that your periods have stopped or are irregular, you are unlikely to conceive until your weight is more normal.

■ If you are overweight, you are at risk of raised blood pressure, which may be a problem in late pregnancy. You may also be at risk from "gestational" diabetes, that is, diabetes developed during pregnancy. The extra weight can also put an increased strain on your joints during pregnancy and lead to a worsening of common problems such as backache and breathlessness.

■ Dieting during pregnancy is not normally recommended, so if you need to lose weight, do so before you try to conceive. You should aim to lose weight slowly and steadily by following a healthy eating plan and by taking moderate exercise. Avoid crash weight-loss diets as these may deprive your body of essential nutrients and harm your health. Ask your doctor or a dietician for further advice.

■ If you are seriously underweight or suffer from an eating disorder such as bulimia or anorexia, seek professional advice, as these conditions can cause growth problems in the developing foetus.

RESPONSIBLE FATHERHOOD

Smoking or moderate to heavy drinking may cause fertility problems and your partner's health may be harmed by her breathing in your cigarette smoke. Fathers who drink heavily also have a higher risk of producing a child with fetal alcohol syndrome. Like your partner, you should give up smoking and stop drinking or reduce your alcohol intake before you try to conceive.

CONCEPTION

If you and your partner have been following the preconception guidelines in this section (see pp. 6–11) for at least three months before trying to conceive, you have given yourself an excellent chance of conceiving and producing a healthy baby.

FOR A PREGNANCY TO OCCUR

- The woman must be ovulating (see right).
- Intercourse must take place within 48 hours of ovulation.
- There must be an adequate number of good-quality active sperm reaching the egg, including one to fertilize it.
- There must not be any barrier to prevent fertilization taking place.
- Once fertilization has occurred, the developing embryo needs to become successfully embedded in the prepared lining of the uterus.

OVERCOMING PROBLEMS WITH CONCEPTION

Don't be disappointed if conception does not occur immediately after you have unprotected intercourse. Studies have found that only one in four perfectly normal couples conceive within a month. If after trying to become pregnant for a year you are still unsuccessful, talk to your doctor who can arrange tests. These can include semen analysis, ultrasound or checking the fallopian tubes for blockages or abnormality with dye (hysterosalpingogram) or with a tiny camera called a laparoscope.

RESPONSIBLE FATHERHOOD

Tight trousers or underwear can raise the temperature of the testicles and inhibit sperm production, so change to boxer shorts. Follow the general guidelines to help conception such as eating healthily, reducing obesity, and stopping smoking.

WHEN DO YOU OVULATE?

A woman is born with about 250,000 to 400,000 immature eggs (ova) in each ovary. About 14 days before a period is due an egg ripens and is released into the fallopian tube. This is known as ovulation. Once the egg is released it lives for up to 24 hours, although a sperm can live inside a woman's body for up to 72 hours. The menstrual cycle generally averages 28 days, but many women have irregular cycles, irregular ovulation, or other problems. So establishing that ovulation takes place and pinpointing when, can be crucial to successful conception. This can be done by:

■ **Basal body temperature monitoring – the "temperature method"**

Record your temperature on a chart every day over the course of a month. After ovulation has occurred, the body temperature rises by up to 0.5°C (1°F). As the temperature rises only after ovulation has taken place, it cannot be used to detect ovulation, and intercourse must take place as soon as possible after the rise has been noted. Difficulties in reading and interpretation can impair the reliability of this method.

■ **Cervical mucus changes**

At the beginning and end of the cycle, the mucus is scant, sticky and opaque. As the oestrogen level peaks, just before ovulation, it gets slick and glassy. This fertile mucus is favourable to the sperm and so to fertilization. This information is often used in conjunction with the temperature method.

■ **Home ovulation prediction tests**

Prior to ovulation, the amount of a substance known as luteinizing hormone (LH) in a woman's body increases sharply. Home ovulation prediction tests work by detecting the amount of LH in a woman's urine on a number of days during her menstrual cycle – a definite increase shows that the time of peak fertility is approaching. Having sexual intercourse in the two to three days following the detection of the LH surge will improve your chances of becoming pregnant. These home prediction tests are available from pharmacies.

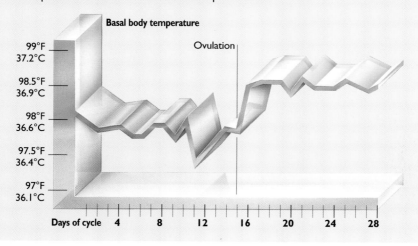

SIGNS OF PREGNANCY

There are a number of signs and symptoms that can indicate that you are pregnant. You may not notice all of them at first, or you may know you are pregnant because you "feel different". A missed period is the most obvious sign that you are pregnant, especially if your periods are usually regular. But there may be other early indications, including a frequent need to pass urine and tender or enlarged breasts.

Sensitivity to smells
You may have an increased sensitivity to strong smells, such as cigarette smoke or certain foods, and they may make you feel sick.

Breast changes
High levels of progesterone (see p. 23) may make your breasts feel heavy and tender. Your nipples may also become slightly darker.

Missed periods
A period is a sign that the womb does not need the extra lining it has prepared in case it needs to receive a fertilized egg. So a missed period may mean that fertilization has taken place.

Frequent need to pass urine
This is due to the hormone relaxin (see p. 23) relaxing the bladder muscles, combined with increased fluids in the body and increased urine production.

Fatigue
You may feel very tired due to the rapidly growing placenta and foetus.

Taste changes
Hormonal changes may make some foods distasteful, or leave a metallic taste in the mouth. You may also start to crave certain foods.

Morning sickness
High levels of of the hormone HCG (see p. 23), increased stomach acid and an increased sensitivity to smells may contribute to nausea and vomiting.

Increased vaginal discharge
This is due to hormonal changes.

CONFIRMING THE PREGNANCY

■ Early confirmation of pregnancy is important so that you can make any necessary changes to your lifestyle as soon as possible. If your pregnancy is planned, you should already be eating healthily, exercising regularly and working to cut out any bad habits such as smoking or drinking. If your pregnancy is not planned, it is important to make these changes now.

■ If your period is late and you have any of the other signs of pregnancy described opposite, a urine or blood test can be carried out to confirm the diagnosis.

■ You can do a urine test yourself at home, using a kit that you can buy from your local pharmacist. Alternatively, it can be carried out at a women's health clinic or by a doctor.

■ Your doctor may also offer you a blood test. This is more sophisticated than a urine test and measures precisely the amount of the hormone human chorionic gonadotrophin (HCG, see p. 23) circulating in the blood. As the amount of HCG varies throughout pregnancy, it also helps to pinpoint the date when conception occurred and to predict when your baby is due (see p. 20 for more details of this).

■ Once you are more than six weeks pregnant, your doctor may follow a urine or blood test with a medical examination. He or she may examine the uterus, which will feel enlarged and softened, by gently pressing your abdomen or by an internal examination.

HOME-TESTING KITS

Your pregnancy can be diagnosed from the first day of your missed period (about two weeks after conception if you have a regular menstrual cycle) using a pregnancy testing kit. These are simple and quick to use and can be bought from your pharmacist.

■ It is best to test your urine first thing in the morning before you have drunk anything, since this is usually the time that the urine contains the highest amount of HCG.

■ If the instructions are followed correctly, the test should give an accurate result.

■ Occasionally, a test may give a "false negative"; that is, it may tell you that you are not pregnant even though you are. This is more likely if your periods are irregular.

■ If your result is negative but your period has still not arrived one week later, try the test again.

■ If your urine test is positive, you should make an appointment to see your doctor as soon as possible.

CHOOSING A PRACTITIONER

Now that you are pregnant, you and your partner will need to decide how to prepare for childbirth, where you want the baby delivered and by whom. There are several options available. For instance, do you want your leading carer to be a certified midwife or a doctor? Is the doctor's practice near to your home or work? What is their attitude to your concerns about active childbirth, pain relief in labour, the presence of fathers at the delivery and breastfeeding? When making your decision, think about your basic approach to pregnancy and the style and type of care and delivery that you want.

YOUR FAMILY DOCTOR

Your family doctor, in conjunction with the community midwife, may be able to provide most of your antenatal care, with hospital appointments being necessary only for special tests or if complications arise. The advantage is that your doctor knows you personally and knows your medical history. Not all family doctors offer obstetric care, however, and your doctor may pass you on to another in the same practice who does.

MIDWIFERY CARE

Midwives are highly trained to provide a woman with continuing health care from early pregnancy right through labour, delivery and the early days after birth. Before being allowed to practise, a midwife must, by law, be registered. Most are also trained nurses. A midwife may work in the community with a family doctor, or in a hospital. There are also some independent midwives. A community or independent midwife is likely to get to know you well and help you to plan the kind of care that you would like. Some hospitals are also introducing "one to one" midwifery care. If any complications arise at any time, the midwife will refer you to your family doctor or obstetrician.

CHOOSING AN OBSTETRICIAN

Obstetricians are doctors who specialize in the care of pregnant women, and are trained to handle any complications of pregnancy and delivery. If yours is a high-risk pregnancy (for example, if you have a history of miscarriages, or a medical condition such as diabetes) you will need to see an obstetrician. Even if you have no such complications, you can, if you wish, see an obstetrician from the start. Before choosing an obstetrician, it is best to ask around for a personal recommendation and then discuss this with your doctor. Alternatively, you can ask your doctor to refer you to someone.

CHOOSING THE PLACE OF BIRTH

Choosing the place of birth will inevitably depend to some extent on the choices available in your area or the place from which the obstetrician you have chosen works. This may be a large general hospital with a specialist maternity unit or a birthing room. A birthing room provides a comfortable setting similar to a bedroom or hotel room but is fully equipped to allow a mother to stay in the same bed from labour through delivery to postpartum care. Other alternatives include a birth unit within a small community hospital, a birth centre that is not in or near a consultant unit, or a home birth. Home births are advisable only for low-risk cases and are not normally recommended for first babies.

ANTENATAL CLASSES

Attending an antenatal class can be of great benefit to you and your spouse. At most classes you will learn about the changes to your mind and body you can expect during pregnancy. You will learn what happens during labour so that you can be more prepared and consequently more relaxed and able to deal with pain. And some aspects of early parenthood will usually be covered. Classes offer an opportunity to make new friends and obtain emotional support from other pregnant women. Before deciding which approach is right for you and what class to attend, it is obviously best to read as much as you can and obtain more specific information from the instructor of any class you are thinking of attending.

THE PURPOSE OF ANTENATAL CLASSES

Whether they are called antenatal, childbirth or parentcraft classes, all such classes usually include information about preparation for childbirth, relaxation techniques for coping with labour, the physical process of labour, information about various birth methods and pain relief, and preparation for parenthood. Videos on labour and various birth methods may be shown.

Some classes will discuss early pregnancy concerns such as nutrition, exercises and foetal development – although many women do not start attending antenatal classes until the sixth or seventh month of pregnancy – and all should give you the opportunity to ask questions and voice any worries you may have. If your class is near the hospital where you plan to give birth, you will be able to get more specific information about the practices and facilities there, and arrange a tour of the hospital.

Most classes also encourage partners to attend. If you don't have a partner or your partner is unable or unwilling to attend, you may be able to take a friend or relative along with you if you wish. If you have chosen someone other than your partner to be your birth companion, they will be made welcome at classes.

FINDING THE RIGHT CLASS FOR YOU

Allow yourself enough time to find the right class. Classes may be run by a midwife at a health centre, doctor's surgery or the hospital you are attending for your antenatal care. Or you may prefer a class run by a government or volunteer organization, or by a private childbirth teacher or counsellor. Classes close to where you work may fit your schedule better; those closer to home mean that you will meet parents and babies who are likely to live close by, too, which will make keeping in touch after the birth easier.

Once you've chosen the type of class you want to attend or have heard of one that is good, you may want to reserve a place in advance – if it is very popular, there may not be an immediate vacancy. Classes typically meet once a week for about two hours and last for around eight to ten weeks. Aim to have completed a course with about four weeks to spare before your due date.

TYPES OF CLASSES

You can, if you wish, go to more than one type of class – for example, a yoga or exercise class for pregnant women, as well as a more conventional antenatal one. Or you may prefer one that practises special birth techniques or follows a particular philosophy or school of thought. No childbirth class should promise you a pain-free labour or delivery, but there are several relaxation methods or philosophical approaches available which may help you to avoid or minimize the use of drugs. However, you do not have to follow one approach only. Many classes combine the best elements of various philosophies.

COMMON ANTENATAL APPROACHES

Robert Bradley

This American obstetrician invented the "husband-coached" approach to childbirth, in which the birth partner acts as the woman's coach and supporter in pregnancy. A healthy diet and exercise are emphasized to ease discomforts of pregnancy, and deep breathing is advocated for a drug-free labour.

Fernand Lamaze

Lamaze was a French doctor who developed psychoprophylaxis – an approach centred on techniques of breathing relaxation. He believed that the pain of childbirth was heightened by fear and tension and that pregnant women could be conditioned by practising relaxation techniques to respond to pain in a positive way. The psychoprophylaxis approach has now become more flexible, and women should not feel that something is going wrong if they have pain in labour.

Active birth

This approach, based on yoga, involves moving around and changing positions throughout labour. You give birth in a squatting or kneeling position or on all fours while your birth partner supports you physically. It is important to learn stretching exercises and how to adopt "open" positions.

WHEN IS YOUR BABY DUE?

To calculate when your baby is due, use the calendar below. Look along the top rows to find the first day of your last period; the date below it is your estimated date of delivery (EDD). In the example below, if the first day of your last period was 14 January, then your estimated due date would be 21 October. Remember, though, that only five per cent of babies are born on their due date. It is perfectly normal for babies to be born two weeks before or two weeks after the EDD.

Date of your last period

Estimated date of delivery

| Jan | 1 2 3 4 5 6 7 8 9 10 11 12 13 14 15 16 17 18 19 20 21 22 23 24 25 26 27 28 29 30 31 |
| **Oct** | 8 9 10 11 12 13 14 15 16 17 18 19 20 21 22 23 24 25 26 27 28 29 30 31 1 2 3 4 5 6 7 |

| Feb | 1 2 3 4 5 6 7 8 9 10 11 12 13 14 15 16 17 18 19 20 21 22 23 24 25 26 27 28 |
| **Nov** | 8 9 10 11 12 13 14 15 16 17 18 19 20 21 22 23 24 25 26 27 28 29 30 1 2 3 4 5 |

| March | 1 2 3 4 5 6 7 8 9 10 11 12 13 14 15 16 17 18 19 20 21 22 23 24 25 26 27 28 29 30 31 |
| **Dec** | 6 7 8 9 10 11 12 13 14 15 16 17 18 19 20 21 22 23 24 25 26 27 28 29 30 31 1 2 3 4 5 |

| April | 1 2 3 4 5 6 7 8 9 10 11 12 13 14 15 16 17 18 19 20 21 22 23 24 25 26 27 28 29 30 |
| **Jan** | 6 7 8 9 10 11 12 13 14 15 16 17 18 19 20 21 22 23 24 25 26 27 28 29 30 31 1 2 3 4 |

| May | 1 2 3 4 5 6 7 8 9 10 11 12 13 14 15 16 17 18 19 20 21 22 23 24 25 26 27 28 29 30 31 |
| **Feb** | 5 6 7 8 9 10 11 12 13 14 15 16 17 18 19 20 21 22 23 24 25 26 27 28 1 2 3 4 5 6 7 |

| June | 1 2 3 4 5 6 7 8 9 10 11 12 13 14 15 16 17 18 19 20 21 22 23 24 25 26 27 28 29 30 |
| **March** | 8 9 10 11 12 13 14 15 16 17 18 19 20 21 22 23 24 25 26 27 28 29 30 31 1 2 3 4 5 6 |

| July | 1 2 3 4 5 6 7 8 9 10 11 12 13 14 15 16 17 18 19 20 21 22 23 24 25 26 27 28 29 30 31 |
| **April** | 7 8 9 10 11 12 13 14 15 16 17 18 19 20 21 22 23 24 25 26 27 28 29 30 1 2 3 4 5 6 7 |

| Aug | 1 2 3 4 5 6 7 8 9 10 11 12 13 14 15 16 17 18 19 20 21 22 23 24 25 26 27 28 29 30 31 |
| **May** | 8 9 10 11 12 13 14 15 16 17 18 19 20 21 22 23 24 25 26 27 28 29 30 31 1 2 3 4 5 6 7 |

| Sept | 1 2 3 4 5 6 7 8 9 10 11 12 13 14 15 16 17 18 19 20 21 22 23 24 25 26 27 28 29 30 |
| **June** | 8 9 10 11 12 13 14 15 16 17 18 19 20 21 22 23 24 25 26 27 28 29 30 1 2 3 4 5 6 7 |

| Oct | 1 2 3 4 5 6 7 8 9 10 11 12 13 14 15 16 17 18 19 20 21 22 23 24 25 26 27 28 29 30 31 |
| **July** | 8 9 10 11 12 13 14 15 16 17 18 19 20 21 22 23 24 25 26 27 28 29 30 31 1 2 3 4 5 6 7 |

| Nov | 1 2 3 4 5 6 7 8 9 10 11 12 13 14 15 16 17 18 19 20 21 22 23 24 25 26 27 28 29 30 |
| **Aug** | 8 9 10 11 12 13 14 15 16 17 18 19 20 21 22 23 24 25 26 27 28 29 30 31 1 2 3 4 5 6 |

| Dec | 1 2 3 4 5 6 7 8 9 10 11 12 13 14 15 16 17 18 19 20 21 22 23 24 25 26 27 28 29 30 31 |
| **Sept** | 7 8 9 10 11 12 13 14 15 16 17 18 19 20 21 22 23 24 25 26 27 28 29 30 1 2 3 4 5 6 7 |

Health and Diet

HEALTH AND DIET

Looking after yourself from the very first weeks of pregnancy is the most important thing you can do for the welfare of your baby. If you were planning to get pregnant, you may already have made some changes to your lifestyle. If you haven't, start taking extra care of your health from today.

2

You will find that your body is making its own changes. You will experience some emotional highs and lows and some physical discomforts as your body adjusts to its changing hormone levels. Ways are suggested to help you cope with these.

The most important thing is that you have a happy and relaxed pregnancy, without worrying too much. Knowing that you have taken sensible precautions to keep yourself in good health is the first step towards this.

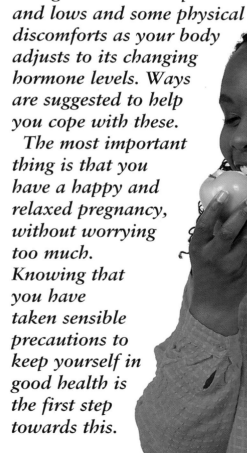

FEELINGS AND HORMONES

Pregnancy is a time of both physical and emotional changes. Some women love being pregnant; others can't wait to get it over with. If this is your first baby, the emotional and physical impact that pregnancy has on your body may be alarming at first. Knowing why these changes are taking place and what to expect can help you to understand what's happening to your body and what you can do to help yourself.

2

FEELINGS AND EMOTIONS

However much you wanted a baby, now that you know you are pregnant you are probably experiencing a mixture of conflicting emotions ranging from elation to apprehension. You may feel thrilled about being pregnant one day, doubtful about it the next. You may be worried about how you will cope as a mother, or about how your partner really feels, or you may burst into tears at the slightest provocation. These emotional highs and lows are perfectly natural, so don't feel guilty about them – many are triggered by an increase in hormones.

In addition to mood swings, rising hormone levels mean you may also experience a number of physical changes. How to cope with these is discussed on pp. 26–27. Once your hormones have stabilized, they may also help you to experience a sense of wellbeing and calmness. In fact, many pregnant women say they have never looked or felt better.

WHAT YOU CAN DO ABOUT NEGATIVE FEELINGS

■ Discuss how you feel with your husband, or with friends or relatives.

■ Have a good cry if you want one.

■ If you are worried about how your life will change, think of the positive benefits that having a child will bring. Acknowledging to yourself that your life will change once you have a child also means that you are being realistic: if you imagine that your life will continue as before, you are deceiving yourself.

■ Read up on pregnancy and parenting, and join an antenatal class so that you are well informed.

■ Things seem worse if you are tired or run down. Keep healthy by doing plenty of exercise, relaxing regularly and eating a balanced diet (see pp. 28–29).

■ If you are seriously depressed or have a lot of worries that you feel you can't solve on your own, seek professional help.

HORMONES

These are chemical substances that are produced by the endocrine glands and released into the bloodstream, where they are carried to different parts of the body. Hormones play a vital part in pregnancy, when their output is greater than at any other time of your life.

THE MAIN PREGNANCY HORMONES

Human chorionic gonadotrophin (HCG)	This hormone is produced by the embryo and prevents menstruation. It also causes the body to produce more progesterone. High levels of HCG during the first three months are thought to be responsible for morning sickness.
Oestrogen and progesterone	These are important in all aspects of pregnancy and control most of the changes that take place. For example, progesterone prepares the lining of the uterus to receive the fertilized egg, stimulates the growth of body tissue and fat and gives you a sense of calmness. Together oestrogen and progesterone stimulate the growth of the milk ducts in the breast, making the breasts swell and the areolae (the area around the nipples) enlarge and darken.
Relaxin	This softens the cervix and relaxes the pelvic muscles and ligaments in preparation for birth.
Oxytocin	This stimulates the uterus to contract and help push out the baby, and after birth it helps the uterus to shrink back to its normal size. It is also responsible for stimulating milk production during breastfeeding.
Prostaglandins	These are local hormone-type substances present in many tissues. They stimulate the uterus to contract, and pessaries or gel containing prostaglandins may be inserted into the vagina to stimulate labour. If your baby is ready to be born, intercourse may start labour, as semen also contains prostaglandins.
Cortisone	The levels of this hormone increase during pregnancy, which is part of the reason that allergic conditions such as asthma and eczema improve at this time.
Adrenalin, noradrenalin and endorphins	These hormones are responsible for increasing the heart rate and also have important effects on mood. Endorphins effect our sense of wellbeing and are the body's natural painkillers. The levels of endorphins in the body increase throughout pregnancy and peak during labour.
Prolactin and Human Placental Lactogen (HPL)	These are both milk-making hormones. They are secreted during pregnancy but oestrogen and progesterone delay milk production. Once the baby is delivered, oestrogen and progesterone levels fall and milk is produced.

2

HEALTH SAFEGUARDS

During pregnancy, your natural immunity to infection may be lowered. Some infections that are usually harmless to people may, during pregnancy, be harmful to your baby's health and development. Although these infections are usually rare, it is wise to take extra precautions to avoid them or protect yourself against them. Some workplaces or occupations may also be harmful during pregnancy.

2

FOOD SAFETY

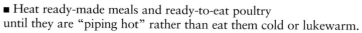

- Avoid raw and undercooked meat and poultry. Be extra careful to wash cutting boards, plates and utensils used for raw meat and poultry thoroughly. Wash your hands carefully after handling these foods.
- Avoid fresh pâté and raw fish, such as sushi.
- Avoid raw eggs and foods containing undercooked egg, such as mayonnaise.
- Refrigerate all cooked and chilled food and dairy products.
- Heat ready-made meals and ready-to-eat poultry until they are "piping hot" rather than eat them cold or lukewarm.
- Do not drink unpasteurized cows', goats' or sheep's milk.
- Avoid soft cheeses with white skin such as Camembert and Brie and the blue-veined varieties such as Stilton, Danish blue, Dolcelatte and Gorgonzola. Other soft cheeses, such as cream cheese and cottage cheese, are safe.

- Avoid soft whip ice cream.
- Wash all fresh fruit, vegetables and salads thoroughly.
- Discard any mouldy foods and sprouting potatoes.

TAKING MEDICATION DURING PREGNANCY

Some medicines can affect the foetus, so do not take any medication without first checking with your doctor. But don't stop taking any prescribed medicines for chronic medical conditions, as a lack of treatment could be more harmful than the drug. Some antibiotics are safe but others can cause bone deformities in the baby. Some anti-bacterial drugs (Sulphonamides) should not be used in late pregnancy and some over the counter pain killers, cough and cold remedies, antacids or iron tablets should also be checked with your doctor. Excessive amounts of vitamins and some herbal remedies can also be dangerous, so discuss these with your doctor.

COPING AT WORK

It is often during the first three months of pregnancy, when you may be battling against morning sickness or tiredness, that you will find it difficult to carry on working normally. If possible, arrange to arrive later and leave earlier. If medical problems such as high blood pressure occur, you may be advised to stop working; otherwise you can continue to work until 28 weeks or longer. But don't push yourself to the limit by rushing around shopping in your lunch break or doing other extra activities. Give yourself plenty of rest breaks where possible, and make sure that you eat a nutritious lunch. You should also keep your legs raised when sitting at a desk. If you have to stand for long periods, wear support pantyhose and vary your position frequently. You should always avoid smoke-filled rooms.

2

AVOIDING INFECTIONS

Listeriosis	If contacted during pregnancy listeriosis can result in miscarriage, stillbirth or severe illness in a newborn baby. High levels of listeria bacteria have been found in foods such as soft cheeses and pâté, and in small amounts in some frozen ready-made meals and ready-to-eat poultry.
Salmonella	This bacteria can cause severe food poisoning and babies may be affected by their mother's high temperature. Salmonella is most frequently found in eggs, poultry and raw meat.
Toxoplasmosis	The toxoplasma parasite can be caught from raw or undercooked meat, cat faeces and infected soil. In a healthy adult it causes influenza-like symptoms, but if caught during pregnancy it may affect the unborn child. If you have already had this infection you will be immune and you can establish this with a blood test. If you are not immune, avoid handling cat litter or if you have to change it yourself, wear gloves, washing the gloves and your hands afterwards. Wash your hands after handling cats and kittens and always wear gloves when gardening and wash your hands afterwards.
Chlamydiosis	Chlamydiosis is a rare disease that may cause pregnant women to miscarry. To avoid infection, do not have contact with sheep during lambing, with milking ewes that have recently given birth, or contact with the afterbirth or new-born lambs.

PHYSICAL CHANGES

You will start noticing changes in your body almost as soon as you know you are pregnant. Hormonal activity increases (see pp. 22–23) as your body naturally prepares itself to nurture you and your baby through the next nine months.

2

BREAST CHANGES

Breast changes start early in pregnancy and by 6–8 weeks your breasts will be noticeably larger. Your nipples and areolae (the circles of darker skin around the nipples) will darken and the veins close to the surface may become larger. Increased progesterone may make your breasts feel firm and tender and you may feel some tingling.

By about 12–14 weeks your breasts may start to produce colostrum, the milk-like substance that will feed your baby for the first few days.

As your breasts grow, wear a good support bra with wide straps. It's better to be measured properly in the last few months. Use breast pads to catch colostrum leaks.

BREATHLESSNESS

As your baby grows and takes up more space, you may become breathless because your lungs do not have as much room to expand. Once your baby's head is engaged (see p.72), you should feel more comfortable again.

To alleviate the problem, sit and stand as straight as possible and sleep propped up in bed.

SKIN CHANGES

The different amounts of hormones may cause some skin changes. These include brown uneven patches on the face (called chloasma); streaks or lines on the breasts, abdomen and thighs (stretch marks); and a dark line running from the top to the bottom of the abdomen. This line, like chloasma marks, becomes worse in the sun, but disappears after pregnancy. Stretch marks fade to a silvery appearance, but never disappear completely. Most health professionals agree that these cannot be prevented by creams, but you may enjoy massaging a good moisturizing cream or oil into your skin.

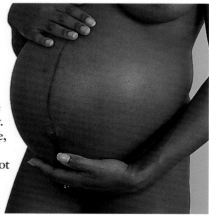

WEIGHT GAIN

The amount of weight women gain during pregnancy varies, but most gain about 10–16.5 kg (22–35 lb). Although you will start to gain weight from the beginning of pregnancy, most of this weight accumulates in the second half. Aim for a moderate, steady weight gain – being seriously underweight or overweight may lead to complications during pregnancy or labour.

COMMON CHANGES

Vaginal discharge is likely to increase in pregnancy. See your doctor if it is smelly, itchy or makes you sore.	■ Wear cotton underwear and panty liners.
Nails may grow faster than usual and become brittle.	■ Use a good nail-conditioning cream. ■ Treat yourself to a professional manicure.
Hair quality and texture often improve during pregnancy, but this is unpredictable.	■ Avoid permanents and chemical colorants.
Tiredness is common during pregnancy, especially during the first three and last three months.	■ Don't overdo things; rest when you can, but also try to take gentle exercise. ■ Eat a well-balanced diet. ■ Accept offers of help. ■ See your doctor or midwife if you feel excessively tired to rule out the possibility of anaemia.
Food aversions and cravings for strange or specific foods are common in pregnancy.	■ Don't worry if your overall diet remains healthy – no single food is vital for health. ■ If you develop an aversion to one food out of a food group (see pp. 28–29), choose a substitute. ■ If you have cravings for non-foods such as soil, see your doctor. Known as pica, these cravings may indicate a nutritional deficiency such as iron.
The need to **urinate frequently** is common during early pregnancy as well as later on, when the enlarged uterus puts pressure on the bladder.	■ Avoid tea and coffee as these are diuretics. ■ Try to empty your bladder as soon as you have the urge. ■ If you have pain or a burning sensation when passing urine, see your doctor in case you have an infection.

2

EATING A HEALTHY DIET

Eating a well-balanced diet during pregnancy should be a pleasure, not a worry. What you eat will become your baby's nourishment, so you need to make sure that you are choosing foods that will build up enough stores of the necessary nutrients from day one of your pregnancy. A healthy diet will help you keep fit and well to meet the demands of pregnancy and labour, and help your body to prepare for breastfeeding your baby if you choose to do so.

2

UNDERSTANDING THE FOOD GROUPS

No one type of food is essential for health and no single food can supply all the nutrients your body needs. A well-balanced diet is one that contains an adequate amount of carbohydrate, protein, fat, vitamins and minerals. These can all be found in the five main food groups, which each have a range of recommended daily servings. If you select a variety of foods and the recommended number of servings from each of these groups, preferably on a daily basis, you are likely to be eating a healthy and balanced diet. If you dislike one type of food from a group – or develop an aversion to it during pregnancy – don't worry, there are always other healthy options to choose from.

CALORIES AND ENERGY

Although you need more energy than usual during pregnancy, your levels of physical activity and your metabolic rate slow down. This compensates for your increased needs. On average, you need to take in only 200–300 more calories a day than were necessary to maintain your pre-pregnancy weight, and this is for the final three months only. If you were underweight at the start of your pregnancy, you may need more calories.

All foods contain calories. But some such as sugar, fat and refined foods are high in calories but low in nutrients. Others, such as grain products or fruit, have relatively few calories, but many nutrients – most of your calories should come from these foods. Base most of your meals around the carbohydrate group on the bottom of the food pyramid shown opposite. These foods are filling without being fattening, contain other nutrients in addition to carbohydrates, and are usually cheap.

To make up the extra calories you can have nourishing snacks between meals. For ideas for healthy snacks, see p. 31.

SPECIAL DIETS

If you follow a vegetarian or vegan diet, discuss this with your doctor, nutritionist or dietician as soon as you know you are pregnant, as you may need vitamin and mineral supplements.

THIS FOOD PYRAMID SHOWS THE
FIVE MAIN GROUPS INTO WHICH
FOODS ARE DIVIDED. USE THE
SHAPE OF THE PYRAMID AS A
GUIDELINE — EAT LESS OF THE
FOODS AT THE TOP AND MORE OF
THOSE AT THE BASE.

2

FATS, SUGAR, SALT AND ALCOHOL

Eat sparingly as these contain few other nutrients.

MEAT, POULTRY, FISH, BEANS AND NUTS

Provide: Protein, vitamins A and B, fibre (nuts and beans), iron and zinc. Servings needed: 2–3 daily (1 serving is 50–70 g/2–3 oz meat or fish, 2 eggs, 2 tbsp peanut butter, ½ cup cooked beans).

DAIRY PRODUCTS

PROVIDE: Calcium, protein, vitamin A (whole milk products), zinc, magnesium and iodine. Servings needed: 2–3 daily. (1 serving is 40 g/1½ oz of cheese, 200 ml/⅓ pint milk or yoghurt, ½ cup cottage cheese).

VEGETABLES

Provide: Fibre, vitamins A and C, folic acid, potassium and iron. Servings needed: 3–5 or more daily. Select one serving from dark yellow or green leafy vegetables for Vitamin A. (1 serving is 1 cup of leafy greens, ½ cup cooked carrots or squash, 175 ml/6 fl oz of juice).

FRUITS

Provide: Fibre, vitamin C, and potassium. Servings needed: 2–4 or more daily. Select one serving from citrus fruits, tomatoes or other fruits rich in vitamin C. (1 serving is 1 medium-sized apple, pear or orange, 90 ml/3 fl oz of fruit juice).

BREAD, CEREAL, PASTA AND RICE

Provide: Protein, fibre, energy, vitamins and minerals.
Foods which contain plenty of fibre include wholemeal bread, baked potatoes and wheat or oat bran breakfast cereals. Breakfast cereals are also usually fortified with vitamins and iron.
Servings needed: 6–11 daily. (1 serving is 1 slice of bread, ½ English muffin or small bagel, 30 g/1oz of cereal, ½ cup cooked rice or pasta).

ESSENTIAL NUTRIENTS

The following lists should help you change your eating habits and find the nutrients you need in familiar, everyday foods.

2

NUTRIENT	NEEDED FOR	GOOD SOURCES
Fibre	Helps prevent constipation and haemorrhoids. Too much can interfere with the absorption of iron and calcium.	Wholemeal bread and pasta, some breakfast cereals, potatoes, fruit, vegetables, beans and pulses.
Calcium	Muscle function, correct functioning of the immune system and building bones and teeth.	Dairy products, dark-green leafy vegetables, eggs and fish. You need at least 1200 mg a day.
Zinc	Growth and development.	Meat, dairy products, oysters, wholemeal bread, cereals, beans and nuts.
Iron	The formation of red blood cells, which carry oxygen to the tissues and foetus. Deficiency leads to anaemia, which causes tiredness and shortness of breath.	Red meat, oily fish (such as tinned sardines and pilchards), fortified breakfast cereals, beans and pulses, pumpkin, dried apricots and leafy green vegetables. Check with your doctor before taking an iron supplement as too much iron can be toxic. Keep iron tablets out of reach of children.
Vitamins	General good health, but necessary only in small quantities.	A balanced diet (see p. 29) should normally provide all you need, but you should take a folic acid supplement (see p. 11) during the first 12 weeks of pregnancy. An excess of Vitamin A may damage your baby.

CHANGING YOUR EATING HABITS

If you already have healthy eating habits, only smalll adjustments need be made to make sure you are taking adequate nutrients. If you are not used to a regular eating pattern, or eat a lot of junk food, try and improve your diet gradually.

■ Try to eat a variety of food from each of the main food groups each day.

■ Try to eat three regular meals a day. If you find this difficult, be flexible about the times and the amount. If you can't face breakfast, for example, have something substantial mid-morning.

■ Have a minimum of six to eight drinks a day. Replace sugary or carbonated drinks and caffeine with water, low-fat milk or herbal teas.

■ Meals don't have to be cooked if you haven't the time. A healthy snack (see below) can be as nourishing as a cooked meal.

■ To avoid eating too much saturated fat, limit full-fat products and have low-fat substitutes instead.

■ Try eating dried fruits as a substitute for sweets.

■ Limit salt in your cooking, avoid salty foods and don't add extra salt to your plate.

■ Avoid processed foods such as pies, crisps, cakes and biscuits, or sweets.

■ Iron is absorbed better by the body if you eat iron-containing foods (such as red meat) with foods containing vitamin C (such as fruit or vegetables). Absorption is also reduced by drinking tea or coffee with a meal.

Healthy snacks

When you feel hungry and don't have time for a meal, try to avoid eating processed or refined foods. Instead, eat a snack that contains nutrients, rather than food with empty calories, such as:

■ A sandwich with a filling such as cheese, oily fish, hard boiled egg, cooked meat and salad, banana and peanut butter

■ Wholemeal toast with a topping such as cream cheese, yeast extract, peanut butter or beans

■ Fresh or dried fruit

■ Raw vegetables with cheese dip or hummus

■ Low-sugar, low-fat "live" yoghurt with added fresh or canned fruit

■ A pizza with salad

■ A baked potato with grated cheese or plain yoghurt

■ Savoury biscuits with cheese

■ A glass of low-fat milk and slice of fruit or carrot cake

■ Cheese cubes and walnuts

■ Wholemeal breakfast cereal with added fruit

PREGNANCY SICKNESS

Nausea and vomiting during the first three to four months of pregnancy are usually known as morning sickness, however, they can happen at any time of the day. Morning sickness may vary from a slight feeling of nausea to actual vomiting. For some women it is the worst aspect of their pregnancy, but not all women suffer from it and those who do can usually expect it to disappear by 12 to 14 weeks.

2

CAUSES

Pregnancy sickness is thought to be caused by the hormone HCG which rises during the first three months of pregnancy (see p. 23). As HCG levels fall as the pregnancy progresses, the sickness usually lessens. For a minority of women, however, feeling sick lasts throughout pregnancy.

Other trigger factors may be stress, strong smells, iron tablets in the first three months of pregnancy, indigestion, and seeing or smelling food to which you are averse.

If you are excessively sick or your sickness persists after 16 weeks, consult your doctor or midwife.

ALTERNATIVE THERAPIES

Wearing wrist bands, which work on the acupuncture principle, or taking homeopathic remedies such as Ipecacuanha or Nux vomica, may be effective in combating nausea.

Warning!
Severe or excessive vomiting during pregnancy, when a woman is unable to keep any food down and loses weight, is known as hyperemesis gravidarum. It occurs in about one in 200 pregnancies and must be treated by a doctor. Treatment for hyperemesis gravidarum is usually fast and effective and the mother and baby are unlikely to suffer any lasting effects. In rare cases, admission to hospital may be necessary.

WHAT YOU CAN DO

There are many simple remedies to help you to cope with pregnancy sickness. Try some of the suggestions below to see what works for you. If you vomit often, brush your teeth frequently – vomit contains acid which attacks teeth and brushing will help to prevent dental decay.

- Give yourself extra time to get somewhere without rushing.
- Eat any food you like as soon as you're hungry.
- Eat whatever will stay down.
- Eat small snacks of carbohydrate foods such as toast, fruit, dry crackers or plain cooked potato, little and often.

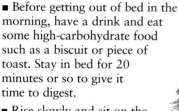

- Avoid fatty foods and foods to which you have an aversion, and don't cook foods with strong smells.
- Try eating foods high in vitamin B6: these include bananas, tuna, potatoes, wheat bran, raisins and sesame seeds.
- Try sucking mints, barley sugar or ginger candy; or chew peppermint-flavoured gum.
- Avoid medication unless prescribed.
- If citrus juices or water upset you, try carbonated drinks, such as spring water, or herbal teas, including peppermint, camomile or fennel.
- Before getting out of bed in the morning, have a drink and eat some high-carbohydrate food such as a biscuit or piece of toast. Stay in bed for 20 minutes or so to give it time to digest.
- Rise slowly and sit on the edge of the bed for a couple of minutes before standing up.

2

MINOR DISCOMFORTS

Most pregnant women experience minor discomforts or ailments at some stage of their pregnancy. Attention to overall health and fitness can minimize the impact of many of them, although few women escape them completely. Occasionally, a symptom may be a sign of a more serious problem so you should always consult your doctor or midwife if you are concerned about your health, or if a problem does not clear up after trying the simple self-help measures.

2

ACHES AND PAINS

These are common mainly because of the effect of hormones loosening the joints, and the ligaments being stretched and strained by your growing baby. Rib pain is caused by the growing uterus pushing the ribs up.

To relieve rib pain, stretch both arms above your head.

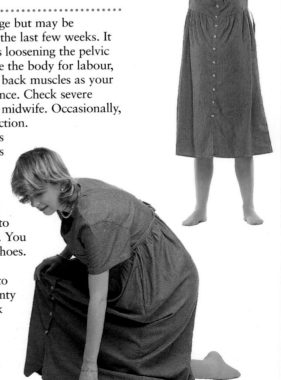

BACKACHE

Backache can occur at any stage but may be especially troublesome during the last few weeks. It is usually due to the hormones loosening the pelvic joints and ligaments to prepare the body for labour, combined with strain on your back muscles as your growing baby alters your balance. Check severe backache with your doctor or midwife. Occasionally, it may be due to a kidney infection.

To prevent backache, always squat or bend from your knees to pick things up and avoid lifting heavy objects. When sitting, support the hollow of your back with a cushion and when standing, pay attention to your posture and stand "tall". You should also wear low-heeled shoes.

If you are suffering from backache, apply heat or cold to the affected area and have plenty of rest; have a massage, or ask your doctor, midwife or physiotherapist about special back exercises. Many women have found that yoga helps to relieve backache.

VARICOSE VEINS

These are due to increased weight and the effects of hormones and although they are not serious, they may cause aching or sore legs. To help avoid them, don't stand for long periods and sit with your feet up whenever possible. Support tights may also be helpful, but should be put on before you get out of bed in the morning.

Varicose veins of the vulva are not uncommon. If you suffer from these, raise the foot of the bed slightly to take pressure off your genitals.

SWOLLEN FEET AND ANKLES

Oedema, or swelling of the feet and ankles, may occur because fluid is retained more easily in pregnancy, particularly at the end of the day and in hot weather. To alleviate the swelling, try foot circles (p. 54), avoid standing or sitting for long periods, wear support tights and comfortable shoes and rest with your legs up whenever possible. Always mention any swelling in the hands and face to your doctor, as this could be a sign of pre-eclampsia.

ITCHING

Itching caused by the stretched abdominal skin is common in late pregnancy. Apply a cream for dry skin or calamine lotion and avoid using soap. Wear light clothes in natural fabrics, choosing several layers in cold weather, and avoid anything stretchy like lycra next to your abdomen. In rare cases it may be caused by a liver problem so consult your doctor or midwife if itching is excessive or if your skin looks yellow.

OTHER AILMENTS
There are a number of other ailments that you may become concerned about as your pregnancy progresses. Many of these are easily explained and quickly relieved, however, if a problem persists, see your doctor.

2

AILMENT	WHAT TO DO
Faintness can occur if your blood pressure drops due to a sudden change of position, or drop in blood sugar level. You may also feel faint when lying on your back in late pregnancy.	■ Get up slowly after sitting or lying down, loosen any tight clothing and place a cool damp cloth on your forehead. ■ Avoid lying on your back in late pregnancy. ■ Avoid long periods without food, as this can cause a drop in blood sugar. ■ Avoid sugary food. Have a healthy snack such as a sandwich or a banana (see p. 31).
Nose bleeds occur because there is an increased supply of blood to the nose during pregnancy.	■ Gently squeeze your nostrils together, just below the bony bridge of the nose for at least 5–10 minutes. ■ If your nasal passages are dry, gently apply petroleum jelly on a cotton bud. ■ If bleeding is persistent, consult your doctor.
Sinuses are more sensitive and can swell, causing headaches and nasal congestion.	■ Try a steam inhalation to help relieve congestion, adding one or two drops of eucalyptus or peppermint oil.
Indigestion and heartburn are mainly due to hormones relaxing the stomach muscles. These are often worse at night or when lying down.	■ Try to identify which foods are causing the problem and avoid them. ■ Eat small but frequent meals. ■ Avoid highly spiced, very cold, or fried foods. ■ Sit up straight while eating and sleep propped up. ■ Ask your doctor about antacids.
Tingling and numbness in the hands is usually due to the growing uterus resting on nerves.	■ Change your position or raise your hands above your head. ■ Try hanging a numbed hand over the side of the bed or shaking it vigorously.
Headaches may occur more often than usual during pregnancy, probably due to hormonal factors.	■ Take a walk. ■ Try relaxation techniques (see pp. 58-61). ■ If necessary, ask your doctor to recommend a safe painkiller. If your headaches are severe or accompanied by vomiting or oedema, contact your doctor.

AILMENT	WHAT TO DO
Stress incontinence is leakage of urine when you laugh, cough, or sneeze. It is caused by weak pelvic floor muscles. It may occur during the last months of pregnancy or following delivery.	■ Do pelvic floor exercises (see p. 55). ■ Wear a sanitary pad or panty liner if necessary. ■ Urinate as soon as you feel the urge to do so. ■ Try to empty your bladder completely: to do this, sit or lean forward on the toilet.
Muscle cramp is probably due to chemical and hormonal changes in the body.	■ Avoid pointing the toes when stretching your legs as this can trigger cramp. ■ Gently massaging your calf muscles in the bath before bedtime may help night time cramps. ■ If a spasm occurs, pull your feet toward your face with your leg straight. ■ Massage your legs.
Pelvic pain is due to the loosening and stretching of the ligaments.	■ Lie down. ■ Have a warm bath. ■ Ask your partner to massage the area. ■ Try some gentle exercises (see pp. 54-55). ■ Consult your doctor or midwife about severe pelvic or abdominal pain. If pelvic pains are severe, you may need complete rest.
Constipation is common and probably due to the effect of the hormone progesterone. During later months, pressure from the enlarged uterus on the bowels can make the problem worse.	■ Make sure your diet contains plenty of high-fibre foods (see p. 30). ■ Drink plenty of fluids (especially water and fruit juices). ■ Exercise daily: a brisk walk, pelvic floor and other safe pregnancy exercises will help. ■ If the problem persists, ask your doctor or midwife to recommend a mild laxative.
Haemorrhoids (piles) are swollen veins in and around the rectum and are common in pregnancy. Symptoms include itching, soreness, pain when opening the bowels and bleeding. They are worsened by constipation.	■ Avoid constipation (see above). ■ Stop smoking. ■ Take regular exercise and practise relaxation. ■ Use warm water or moist tissues instead of paper to wipe yourself. ■ Apply a soft cold compress of witch hazel, Epsom salts or an ice pack. ■ Try a haemorrhoid cream or suppository. ■ Always have bleeding from the rectum checked by your doctor.

2

GETTING BIGGER

As your body continues to grow, being comfortable can sometimes pose problems. Some of your clothes and shoes will start to feel tight and you may wonder what to wear. An increasing girth can also make finding a comfortable sleeping position difficult. But there are several measures you can take to help you stay comfortable and to continue looking good throughout pregnancy.

2

WHAT TO WEAR

■ Up to around five months you probably won't need to buy any special clothes for your pregnancy. Many of your normal clothes will be wearable if they are loose or have elasticated waists.

■ Wear loose cotton tops, such as baggy T-shirts and sweaters, skirts with elasticated waists and loose-fitting dresses or borrow your spouse's shirts, sweaters and shorts, which are cut big and baggy.

■ Tight clothing will not harm your baby, but constricted clothing around the waist will be uncomfortable for you, and as your size increases, may restrict your breathing and make you feel faint. Avoid, too, clothes that restrict the blood flow to your legs, such as knee-high socks or tight underwear.

■ You will tend to feel the heat more than usual, so light-weight loose-fitting clothes made of cotton or other natural materials are best. If it is cold, wear several layers.

■ Shoes with a low heel are better for your back and for your overall posture than totally flat shoes or high-heeled shoes, which can be dangerous. After five or six months you may find that you need a wider shoe or shoes half a size bigger. Shoes made of natural material such as leather or canvas allow your feet to breathe.

■ Replace elastic in the waist of comfortable tracksuit style trousers or skirts with a cord that can be loosened as your waist expands.

■ It is worth asking friends who have had babies if they have any cast offs (one-off purchases like a jacket, a smart dress for a party, or a swimsuit are easy to pass on).

WHAT TO BUY

- 2–3 well-fitting support bras/nursing bras if you are going to breastfeed. Ask to be measured for these – it is quite difficult to judge for yourself how big you might get when your milk comes in.

- 1–2 pairs of shoes ½-size larger or wider (especially if the last months of your pregnancy are in summer).

- 2–3 front-opening nightdresses/pairs of pyjamas if you are going to breastfeed (you will need these in hospital).

- Buy extra-large pantyhose or support tights instead of the more expensive maternity tights.

- Bikini-style panties that can be worn under your bump, or large, stretchy ones that you can pull up over it are more comfortable than regular ones. Cotton panties or at least panties with a cotton gusset are best.

- Buy clothes such as dresses and bras with a front opening for breastfeeding, so that you can get some wear out of them after pregnancy.

- Several mail-order companies specialize in maternity wear and offer good value-for-money because everything is coordinated: a pair of trousers or leggings, skirt, dress and a couple of T-shirts, for example, offers enormous scope for mixing and matching.

GETTING YOUR REST

During the last months of pregnancy you may find sleeping more difficult as a comfortable position can be hard to find. In addition, the extra weight you are carrying around may also make you feel very tired. To help sleeplessness and exhaustion:

- Try a warm bath at bedtime with a few drops of lavender oil added to help you relax.

- Take short "cat naps" or rest during the day.

- Practise your relaxation techniques.

- Try lying on your side with one leg bent and a pillow supporting your knee. You could also place a pillow under your abdomen if this is more comfortable.

TRAVELLING

It is generally safe to travel during pregnancy, but sometimes it can be quite exhausting. If you are going to travel over long distances plan your journey carefully. In the first three months (first trimester), you may suffer from nausea or vomiting, and throughout pregnancy, the need to urinate frequently can be a problem on long journeys.

The most comfortable time for long-distance travel is during the second three months (second trimester). By this time your body will have adjusted to pregnancy, and you will feel at your fittest and best. Morning sickness is usually no longer a problem and you will probably have more stamina for sitting for long periods of time.

2

WHAT TO TAKE

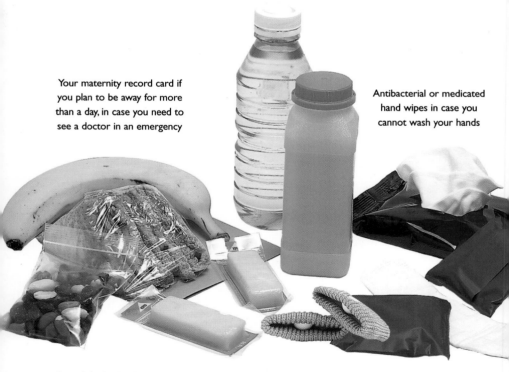

Your maternity record card if you plan to be away for more than a day, in case you need to see a doctor in an emergency

Antibacterial or medicated hand wipes in case you cannot wash your hands

Some light but healthy snacks and fluids, so that food and drink is readily available if you need it (see p. 31).

Travel bands in case of nausea

Light sanitary pads or panty liners if you have a heavy vaginal discharge or stress incontinence

DRIVING

When you travel by car it is essential to wear a correctly fitted seat belt. A seat belt worn high across the abdomen can be dangerous to you and your baby in the event of an accident. The safest way to wear a seat belt is with the shoulder harness between the breasts and the lap belt across the thighs so that it fits under the abdomen. Try to avoid driving during rush hour so that you are not breathing in heavy fumes. On long trips, try to take short stops every hour or two, and walk around to stretch your legs. In the second or third trimester, do not undertake anything longer than a three hour drive if you are driving alone.

AIR TRAVEL

If you plan to travel late in your pregnancy, check with your doctor about the chance of premature labour. Most airlines limit their flights to women no closer than four weeks from their due date. The metal detectors used for airline security checks are not harmful to the foetus. Feet can swell when travelling by air even if you are not pregnant, so make extra sure your shoes are not too tight. Walk around and stretch frequently.

GENERAL TIPS

- Try to divide up long journeys into shorter manageable sections.
- Wear loose comfortable clothes that do not restrict you.
- Remember to empty your bladder frequently.
- Do not take any travel-sickness pills without first checking with your pharmacist or doctor that they are safe.
- If you plan to be away from home for some time you may need to register temporarily with another doctor in your new area.
- If you are travelling abroad, ask your doctor what vaccinations are necessary, and whether these are safe during pregnancy. If possible, avoid visiting a country where infectious diseases such as malaria or cholera are prevalent.

REMINDERS

Being healthy before you conceive – and staying healthy during pregnancy – will give your baby the best possible start in life. Use this list as a reminder of what to do before and after conception to make sure you and your baby get all the nutrients you need, and avoid as many potential hazards as possible.

WHEN YOU ARE TRYING TO CONCEIVE

■ Take a daily folic acid supplement (at least 400 micrograms/0.4mg) in the three months before you plan to conceive and during the first 12 weeks of pregnancy.

■ Check whether you are immune to rubella (German measles).

■ Ask your doctor's advice on whether to seek genetic screening or other tests.

■ Cut out smoking and recreational drugs, and limit your alcohol intake.

WHEN YOU BECOME PREGNANT

■ Avoid alcohol, or severely limit your intake.

■ Don't smoke and avoid smoky rooms.

■ If you need an x-ray, make sure you tell the technician you are pregnant.

■ Don't take any unprescribed medicines, vitamin or mineral supplements, herbal remedies or herbal teas containing aloe, coltsfoot, heart's ease, licorice, nutmeg, pennyroyal, sassafras and tansy.

■ Avoid contact with people suffering from infectious diseases.

■ Avoid contact with chemicals, lead paint and other toxic materials; don't mix household cleaners containing ammonia with those containing chlorine.

■ Wear gloves when changing cat litter or when gardening; avoid contact with sheep and lambs during lambing season.

■ Eat a well-balanced diet. Take extra care when storing and preparing food.

■ Wash fruit and vegetables thoroughly, even those sold as "ready washed".

■ Avoid eating raw or lightly cooked eggs or food containing these products.

■ Don't eat liver or liver products, such as fresh pâté and liver sausage.

■ Don't take fish oil supplements.

■ Don't eat unripened cheeses such as Brie, Camembert and blue-vein cheeses.

■ Don't eat food that has passed its sell-by date.

■ Reduce your intake of sugary carbonated drinks and caffeine (coffee, tea, chocolate and cola).

■ Cook all foods until they are hot right through.

■ Wear a correctly fitted seat belt when travelling by car.

■ Consult your doctor if you feel unwell, start bleeding after your pregnancy has been confirmed, suffer prolonged or severe pregnancy sickness, or are worried in any way.

Exercise and Relaxation

EXERCISE AND RELAXATION

Regular exercise and adequate rest combined with a well-balanced diet will help you maintain good health for the duration of your pregnancy. Exercise improves your circulation, makes you supple, gives you stamina and improves muscle tone. Appropriate exercise before conception and during pregnancy will help to limit your weight gain, reduce backache, may minimize stretchmarks and lead to a quicker post-natal recovery. Improvements to your circulation will reduce or help to alleviate such common problems as varicose veins, constipation and raised blood pressure. The exercises on the following pages will help you tone up before, during and after pregnancy.

Stress and tension are bad for you and may communicate themselves to your baby. They cause headaches, tightening of the muscles and backache. Exercise will help you to relax, but learning breathing and specific relaxation techniques will be invaluable in helping you breathe correctly and help control pain during labour and delivery.

3

GETTING FIT

3

Women who are fit tend to cope better with pregnancy and labour than those who are not. If you make exercise part of your life before you conceive, you are more likely to continue with it when you are pregnant. In the three months before you conceive, build regular exercise – at least three times a week – into your daily routine. Consult your doctor first if you have been ill or have a physical disability. If you are already pregnant, consult your doctor before taking up anything new.

WHAT KIND OF EXERCISE?

Remember, you are more likely to stick to a prepregnancy exercise programme if you are doing something you enjoy.

■ Moderate exercise such as half an hour's brisk walking a day is beneficial: walk to work, or walk a couple of stops before taking the bus or train.

■ Take up a sport you enjoyed at school, or one you've always wanted to learn. Consider swimming, tennis, golf or an aerobics, yoga or stretch class.

■ Go for a bicycle ride (or try an exercise bike at a gym; if you like it, consider buying one).

■ Do some gardening. Offer to take your neighbour's dog for a walk, or play ball with a friend's or neighbour's child.

■ Buy a rope and skip in the garden.

■ Join a dance class or put on a favourite record and dance around the room.

EXERCISING SAFELY

■ Check with your doctor before starting any exercise regime.

■ Take it easy to start with; and always warm up before you start and cool down when you have finished.

■ Don't exercise on a full or empty stomach: have a high carbohydrate snack, such as a banana or some rice cakes, about half an hour before you start.

■ Make sure your exercise teacher is qualified; ask to see credentials.

■ Always use the right kind of shoes and equipment; wear loose clothing.

■ Never push yourself to the limits. Stop if you feel breathless, exhausted or are in pain.

■ If it's effective, exercise will make you sweat; be sure to drink plenty of fluids.

BASIC EXERCISE POSITION

Poor posture can lead to damaged muscles when you exercise. In addition, learning the "feel" of good posture now will pay dividends when you are pregnant, when your changing shape will throw your body out of alignment. When exercising, check that:

■ You are standing with your feet shoulder-width apart (unless suggested otherwise) and your toes pointing slightly outward.

■ Your stomach muscles are pulled in.

■ Your shoulders are relaxed and down.

■ Your knees are over your feet.

■ Your hips are square to the front and over your knees.

3

PREPREGNANCY EXERCISES FOR STAMINA

Aerobic exercise which gets you nearly out of breath and increases your heart rate helps to build up stamina, improves your circulation and increases your metabolic rate; it also makes you feel good. Some aerobic exercises also improve your overall strength. Good aerobic exercises include:

■ Brisk steady walking — at a rate of 8 km/h (5 mph) — ideally including some hills.

■ Swimming: increase the strength of your arms by wearing webbed gloves to give resistance to the water. If you like swimming, you may also enjoy water aerobics.

■ Jogging; running at a rate of 9.5 km/h (6 mph) is even better.

■ Low-impact aerobic/step/keep fit classes. High-impact aerobics, which can injure your legs, should only be done if you are very fit, and not in pregnancy.

■ Bicycling: indoors or out; this also increases the strength of your legs.

■ Racquet sports such as tennis, badminton and squash.

■ Skipping. Buy a proper sports rope; turning the rope should be effortless.

■ Rowing; this also increases strength in your arms and legs.

EXERCISE IN PREGNANCY

If your pregnancy is progressing normally and without any complications, moderate regular exercise is safe and beneficial to your health. It will improve your circulation, make your muscles stronger and your joints more supple. Exercise can also lessen some of the discomforts of pregnancy such as constipation and fatigue, and helps you relax. If you are physically fit, you are also likely to have an easier pregnancy, labour and post-partum recovery.

GUIDELINES FOR EXERCISE DURING PREGNANCY

Most forms of exercise are safe to continue throughout pregnancy, but it is always worth checking with an obstetric physiotherapist, your midwife or doctor. Always follow the basic guidelines for exercise on page 48. And, in addition, while you are pregnant, it is particularly important to:

■ Avoid jarring and high impact motions. All your muscles are softer than normal during pregnancy and you risk tears or strains. Always check the surface on which you are working for this reason: it should have some give.

■ If you attend exercise classes, make sure your teacher is qualified and knows you are pregnant.

■ Drink little and often to avoid dehydration. Take small, frequent high-carbohydrate snacks, especially if you are suffering from heartburn.

■ Don't exercise in very hot or humid weather or let yourself get too hot. In an effort to cool you down, your body diverts blood from the baby.

■ Always wear a well-fitting support bra designed for exercise. Make sure your shoes are appropriate. Check with an instructor if you are in doubt.

■ Monitor your pulse rate: it should not rise above 140 beats per minute for more than 15 minutes.

3

Warning!

If you have a history of recurrent miscarriage or a complicated pregnancy, exercise should be particularly gentle and moderate. Some women may be advised by their doctor to rest and not to exercise at all.

Stop exercising if you experience any of these symptoms:

■ vaginal bleeding
■ have a leak or gush of amniotic fluid
■ pain of any kind
■ contractions or abdominal pain
■ nausea, dizziness or faintness
■ shortness of breath
■ palpitations or very rapid heart beat

■ any swelling or numbness
■ pain in the legs
■ difficulty in walking
■ persistent headaches
■ visual disturbances
■ decreased foetal movements
■ excessive tiredness

SPORTS IN PREGNANCY

Swimming and water exercise	Swimming is an excellent exercise for your body because it uses many different muscles while the water supports your weight. Women who swim several times a week usually have very strong abdominal muscles after the birth of their baby. You may also enjoy doing some water exercises (aquarobics) as a safe way of maintaining or improving flexibility in pregnancy.
Jogging or running	If you were used to running or jogging before you became pregnant, you can continue in pregnancy. Avoid marathon running or jogging more than 5 km (3 miles) a day. Don't become overheated or too tired and drink plenty of fluids. Make extra sure too, that you wear well-supporting cushioned shoes to prevent jarring, and if possible, jog on soft rather than hard surfaces. As your pregnancy progresses, you may find that jogging becomes more difficult.
Aerobic exercise	If you are used to going to aerobic classes, let the instructor know that you are pregnant. View aerobic exercise in pregnancy as maintaining your fitness, rather than improving it. Don't over exert yourself, work at a pace that allows you to hold a conversation without getting out of breath.
Cycling	If you are comfortable doing so, there is no reason why you should not cycle during pregnancy. The main risk to the baby is from an accident that may cause a miscarriage or premature labour, and towards the end of pregnancy, your shape may make you less stable. Whenever possible, avoid main or busy roads because of the risk of traffic pollution.
Horseriding	Many women go horseriding during pregnancy. Ask your doctor's advice on whether it is suitable for you.
Skating	Jumps should be avoided; otherwise, this can be carried on in a modified form for as long as you can get your skates on!
Skiing	There is a risk of falling with force and harming your baby. Skiing while pregnant is not recommended.
Water sports	Water sports such as water skiing, scuba diving and platform diving are not recommended.

3

STRETCHING

Stretching during pregnancy is both an exercise and a way to relax. Simple stretches should also be used as warm-ups and for cooling down, before and after more vigorous exercise. Stretching can help relieve minor discomforts such as backache and by toning up the muscles and opening up your pelvic area, it will help you to prepare for birth.

GENERAL GUIDELINES

Stretching is generally safe as long as you keep a few points in mind.

■ If you are not used to stretching, work up to it – five minutes a day is fine to start with.

■ Do not jump, bounce or use jerky movements – move smoothly into position.

■ Breathe deeply as you stretch and relax into it.

■ Be aware that the hormone relaxin causes an increased range of movements during pregnancy. As the long-term effects of this are not known, use short stretches rather than progressively increasing your range of movements.

■ Holding a position for your usual length of time may become a strain; if it does, hold briefly and repeat several times.

■ Do not lie flat on your back to stretch from the middle of pregnancy, as the baby may press against a major blood vessel, making you feel faint.

■ Throughout all these movements be aware of your breathing and never hold your breath.

ARM STRETCHING

This helps to lift your ribs off your expanding uterus.

1 Sit in a position that is comfortable: either cross-legged on the floor in the yoga position, or against a wall with your legs straight out in front of you.

2 Place your hands on your shoulders then lift both hands above your head.

3 Stretch one arm higher than the other, reaching for the ceiling. Relax and repeat with the other arm. Repeat the exercise ten times.

4 With both arms raised, swing them down to shoulder height, bring your hands back to touch your shoulders and raise your arms again. Repeat ten times.

SHOULDER STRETCH

This can relieve heartburn and tension in your shoulders.

1 Stand up straight. Raise your right arm above your hand and drop it down between your shoulder blades.

2 At the same time bend your left elbow and reach behind with your left hand. Touch or interlock fingers, if you can. (If you can't reach your other hand, try holding a belt or tie between your hands.) Hold for a count of five, breathing normally.

3 Repeat, with your left hand placed over your shoulder.

4 You can increase this stretch by gently pressing down on your elbow.

3

THE CAT STRETCH

This eases tension in your back and shoulders.

1 Kneel on the floor. Bend forward from the hips with your head down. Slowly "walk" your hands forward so that your arms are extended in front of you. Without arching your back, hold for a count of five, breathing normally.

2 Slowly sink down toward your thighs so that your bottom rests on your heels. Repeat three or four times, then sit up slowly.

GENTLE EXERCISES

If you don't want to, or are unable to, do any sports, attend exercise classes, or actively exercise, there are still some gentle exercises you can do to keep fit, supple and toned during pregnancy. Unless otherwise stated, these exercises can be done throughout pregnancy, but as your baby grows you will become more breathless; and particularly during the last two to three months your mobility and balance will change. Choose exercises that do not aggravate any of these conditions.

INNER THIGH STRETCH

Strong, supple thighs will help to keep you mobile and are essential if you want to deliver your baby in a standing or semi-squatting position.

1 Sit on the floor with your back straight, legs as far apart as you can comfortably get them, and shoulders back.

2 Lean forward from the waist and gradually "walk" your hands out in front of you. When you feel mild tension in your inner thighs, hold for a count of five, then relax. Return to an upright position and repeat three times.

THIGH RAISES

This will also strengthen your thighs and improve your overall mobility.

1 Lie on your side with your lower leg slightly bent at the knee. Support your head on your elbow.

2 Gradually raise your upper leg. Keep it straight but do not lock your knee. When it is as high as is comfortable, hold for a count of five, then lower it. Repeat three times, then repeat on your other side.

3

SQUATTING

This exercises the pelvic muscles and strengthens the inner thighs. It is a good position to practise for labour, and to adopt when doing pelvic floor exercises. As you grow bigger or if you have difficulty in keeping your balance, support yourself by holding the seat of a chair or the edge of a bed.

1 Stand with your feet shoulder width apart. Bending down at your hips and knees, slowly ease yourself into a squatting position.

2 Keeping your back straight and your feet flat on the floor, hold for up to 30 seconds if you can.

3

INNER THIGH STRETCH

This stretches the inner thigh muscles and increases the mobility of your pelvis and hip joints.

1 Sit on the floor with your back straight. Bring the soles of your feet together and let your knees drop toward the ground.

2 Hold your ankles and relax your hips so that your knees are even closer to the floor. Hold for a few seconds, extending these for a few seconds longer as it gets easier. Try to do once or twice a day.

UPPER BODY STRETCH

1 Sit on the floor with your legs wide apart. Bend your left knee and tuck your left foot in to your body. Touch your right foot with your right fingers.

2 Breathe in as you raise your left arm above your head and reach toward your right foot. When you feel mild tension in your side, hold for a count of five.

ABDOMINAL EXERCISES

Du ring pregnancy, your abdominal muscles, which run from your breastbone down to your pubic bone, take most of the extra weight of the baby. If these are flabby, your back muscles have to work harder to protect your spine, which in turn can cause backache. Strong, well-toned abdominal muscles during pregnancy not only help to protect your back, but will also return to condition more quickly after the birth.

CURL-UPS (FOR THE FIRST 3 TO 4 MONTHS ONLY)

These strengthen your abdominal muscles. Never do curl- or sit-ups with your legs straight during pregnancy.

1 Lie on your back with your knees bent and feet flat on the floor. Place your hands behind your head. Breathe in.

2 Breathe out as you pull in your stomach muscles and slowly lift your head, shoulders and upper back off the floor. Hold for the count of two, then slowly lower yourself back on the floor. Repeat five to ten times.

3 If this is difficult, you may find it easier to rest your arms on your thighs and inhale. As you exhale, move your arms toward your knees, at the same time lifting your head and shoulders off the floor. Roll back slowly and repeat five to ten times.

KNEELING PELVIC TILT

1 Kneel on the floor with your hands directly under your hips, and your back flat on the floor.

2 Tighten your abdominal and buttock muscles, and breathing out, gently tilt your pelvis forward and hump up your back. Hold this position for a few seconds, then relax.

STANDING PELVIC TILT

This exercise, which helps you move your pelvis with ease, is a good preparation for labour. It also tones your abdominal muscles and is helpful if you suffer from backache. You can do this exercise in a kneeling, sitting or standing position. You can also roll your hips in a gentle circular movement.

1 Stand with feet well apart and knees directly over ankles, and place one hand on your lower back, and another under your "bump".

2 Drawing in your abdominal and buttock muscles, gently rock your pelvis back and forth.

POSTURE DURING PREGNANCY

Poor posture during pregnancy – when your bottom sticks out and your back hollows – can lead to low backache and unnecessary strain on your body. Poor posture is aggravated by wearing high-heeled shoes or unlaced trainers, and by carrying a bag over the same shoulder, or a child on the same hip, all the time. A bra that offers inadequate support may make you round your shoulders as your breasts become heavier. Be fitted for a good bra.

Good posture involves using your abdominal and buttock muscles to support your baby.

Stand with your feet evenly planted, about hip-width apart and in line with each other. Keep your knees loose and directly over your ankles. Let your shoulders drop down and your arms hang loosely from your sides.

Visualize a string attached to the top of your head and pulling upward through your spine and neck so that your spine is straight and upright. Pull in your abdominal muscles so that your baby nestles toward your spine, rather than sitting out in front of you.

Keep remembering to check your posture and pull your abdominal muscles in.

3

Warning!
After every exercise session, or after exercises which involve lying on the floor, lie down and relax for a few minutes as shown on page 61. Then get up slowly, using your hands to push to a kneeling or sitting position first. If you lie on a bed, turn onto your side and keeping your legs together swing them over the side.

OTHER "EASY" EXERCISES

Even if you are not used to exercising, if your activity is restricted or your work involves long periods of sitting, you still need to try to keep toned and supple. Remember to do the pelvic floor exercises daily (see right), which can be done at any time and any place, but also try some or all of the following other exercises – do whatever suits you. For example, if you cannot go for a walk, try walking or marching on the spot. Remember, though, that aerobic exercise does not have to involve vigorous exercise.

LOW-IMPACT AEROBICS

This builds up your stamina and includes brisk walking, marching on the spot, and swimming.

MARCHING ON THE SPOT

1 Stand in the correct posture for exercising (see p. 45). Start with brisk walking on the spot, lifting your knees and transfering your weight from foot to foot.

2 Increase your pace so that you are "marching". See how high you can lift your knees. Swing your arms freely. Raise your arms up and down, touching each shoulder. Cross them over so that your right arm touches your left knee and vice versa.

3 Take two steps forward and clap your hands on the third. Repeat walking backward.

FOOT AND ANKLE EXERCISES

These can reduce swelling and help circulation.

1 Circle each foot in turn five times in one direction and five in the other.

2 Practise drawing the whole alphabet with your feet, one foot at a time. Keep your legs still but move your ankles.

3

HEAD ROLLS

I Gently let your head bend forward, stretching your neck, hold for a few seconds and lift.

2 Turn it to one side, then face forward, bend head, lift. Repeat with other side in a continual flow. Do not let your head roll back.

SHOULDER ROLLS

I To relieve tension and increase suppleness, slowly circle each shoulder backward several times in turn.

2 Lift both shoulders up, press them gently back and pull them down.

3

PELVIC FLOOR EXERCISES

These are essential but simple and effective exercises which strengthen the muscles around the bladder and vagina and can help to prevent or control stress incontinence before and after delivery. They should be practised several times an hour throughout the day, and are easily done at any time, such as when you are on the telephone, standing, talking, washing dishes, waiting for a bus, etc. To know you have located your muscles, try stopping the flow of urine when you go to the toilet – but do this only to make sure you are practising properly and not as a routine part of the exercise.

I Sit, stand or lie with legs slightly apart.

2 Close and draw up around your back passage as if preventing wind or a bowel action. At the same time, draw in your vaginal muscles as if to grip a tampon or avoid passing urine.

3 Hold tight and count to four, breathing normally. Relax and repeat. Do these as often as possible every day.

AFTER THE BIRTH

Du uring the first few days after birth, as well as facing all the
    excitement and demands of a newborn baby, you may be feeling
sore and exhausted. Exercise is likely to be the last thing you feel like
doing. But exercising to get your shape back is important and is most
successful when it is progressive and gentle. Start right from the first day
after birth, with breathing exercises (see below), foot circles (see p. 54)
and pelvic floor exercises (see pp. 55–57). Pelvic floor exercises are the
most important you can do: practise as often as possible, but at least 30
times a day. They help to stop any urine from leaking, help stitches to
heal and ease perineal pain. They also tighten your vaginal muscles,
which will make intercourse more pleasurable. From the third day after
delivery, add pelvic tilts (see p. 52), leg slides and the pelvic rock. These
exercises can be done even if you have had a caesarean section.

BREATHING EXERCISES

3

This is a gentle way to strengthen your abdominal muscles. Do them three times
before any other exercises.

1 Lie on your bed with your knees bent or sit fully supported in an
armchair. Relax your shoulders, place your hands on your
abdomen so that you can feel it rise, and breathe in slowly and
deeply through your nose.

2 Breathe out slowly
through your
mouth, tightening
your abdominal
muscles as you
do so.

PELVIC ROCK

1 Lie on your back on the bed or floor with
your knees bent and feet flat.

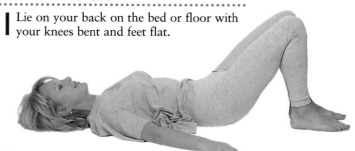

2 Tighten your buttocks, tilt them up, and draw in your abdomen so that the
small of your back rolls flat against the bed or floor. Hold, then relax.

LEG SLIDES

I Lie flat on your back with your knees bent and feet resting on the bed. Breathing in, slide one leg from a bent to a straight position.

2 Breathing out, bend it back again. Repeat with the other leg.

HEAD LIFTS

After about a week, gently move on to more active abdominal exercises.

I Lie on your back with your knees bent, feet flat on the floor and arms by your side. Breathe in and relax your abdomen. Breathing out, lift your head off the floor. Hold for the count of two, then slowly lower your head back.

2 When you feel comfortable doing 10 head lifts, proceed to lifting your shoulders and upper back off the floor, too.

3

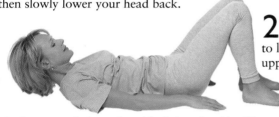

3 Once you feel comfortable doing shoulder lifts, proceed to full curl-ups (see p. 52).

CLOSING THE MUSCLE GAP

During pregnancy, strong abdominal muscles help to carry the extra weight of the baby and support your spine. But unless you were highly toned before you became pregnant, these muscles are likely to have stretched and may have parted by the time your baby is born. Depending on the size of the gap, and the amount of exercise you do, the muscles close together in the first few days or weeks after the birth.

To check for abdominal separation:

■ Lie on your back with your knees bent.

■ Put the fingers of one hand on your abdomen just below your navel and press in gently.

■ Slowly lift your head and shoulders and stretch your other hand forward. If you feel a gap or soft lump the width of a finger or more, the muscles have separated.

To close the gap:

■ Do head lifts (above).

If you can still feel the gap after six weeks, ask a physiotherapist for specific exercises.

RELAXATION TECHNIQUES

Some people find it easier to relax than others. If the basic relaxation exercise on p. 61 does not work for you, there are many other, more formal techniques which pregnant women have found useful. Some of these need to be taught; others can be practised at home.

3

MEDITATION

Meditation involves using your powers of concentration to develop inner calm and relax your body. Practised properly, it can lower blood pressure as well as reducing stress and tension. Although it can be difficult to learn meditation on your own, there are plenty of books and audio cassettes available, or you could go to a teacher of meditation. Ideally you should meditate for 10 to 20 minutes twice a day.

■ Don't eat or drink for about half an hour before meditating.

■ Choose a warm, quiet, dimly lit room.

■ Sit in loose clothes in a comfortable position with your back straight. Try an upright chair or a cushion on the floor.

■ Concentrate on your breathing, an object in the room, or repeat a word or syllable (mantra).

■ If troublesome or stimulating thoughts enter your mind, let them come and go, then resume concentrating on your chosen focus.

YOGA AND T'AI CHI

Yoga is a form of body exercises, posture and breathing which aims to improve overall physical and mental health and wellbeing. In addition to helping you relax during pregnancy, it can also increase your flexibility, lower blood pressure and ease backache. If you already practise yoga, keep it up during pregnancy; if you would like to try it, find an instructor and inform him or her that you are pregnant.

T'ai chi is a "moving" form of meditation which can be relaxing and has the advantage of needing very little physical effort. Again, find an instructor.

MASSAGE

Not only does gentle massage relieve tension and aid relaxation, but it can also alleviate minor discomforts such as headaches and backache. If you can, have a regular massage during pregnancy by a trained masseur or aromatherapist. You could also ask your partner to give you a massage, which is a good way of staying close to each other physically. Or, for a quick stress beater, try massaging your own shoulders.

1 Start with your upper arm and gently knead and squeeze your muscle to loosen any "knots".

2 Use smooth circular movements as you work up your arm to your shoulder.

3 Finally, with your fingertips gently stroke the muscles at the side of your neck into your hairline.

3

AROMATHERAPY

Aromatherapy is the use of essential oils extracted from different parts of plants. It can be used to treat many common conditions including headaches, stress-related problems and insomnia. Essential oils can be massaged into the skin, added to a warm bath, inhaled or used in a hot or cold compress. Aromatherapy can be very beneficial during pregnancy, but consult a trained aromatherapist to be sure that any oils you use are safe for pregnant women.

INSTANT STRESS BEATERS

When it all gets too much, or you are particularly busy but feel you do not have enough time to stop and relax properly, reduce tension in one of these ways.

■ 5–10 minute break: Sit in a comfortable chair or lie on the floor (but do not lie flat on your back during the late stages of pregnancy). Close your eyes and take a deep and slow breath in through your nose and out through your mouth. Systematically tense or stretch all parts of your body, then let go. Try to empty your mind of all thoughts.

■ 2-minute break: Sit on a chair, and breathing slowly and deeply let yourself go limp and floppy like a rag doll.

■ When you have no time: Take a few deep breaths, tense your shoulders up to your ears, hold for a second or two, relax them, then roll them back and forth a few times. Close your eyes and screw up your face by frowning hard. Hold for a few seconds. Slowly relax your face feature by feature.

RELAXATION

However much you are longing to be a parent, pregnancy can be stressful. Not only do you have to cope with the physical and emotional demands on your body of supporting a new life, but you may have other worries, such as pressure at work or financial concerns which can cause stress. Learning to relax or "switch off" is one of the most effective ways of reducing stress. Below are several stress-reducing exercises and strategies you can practise. But always remember, if you are seriously worried or stressed about anything, talking to a professional counsellor may also help.

SIMPLE SWITCHING OFF STRATEGIES

■ Talk to a friend or your spouse; you may be worrying unnecessarily about a problem to which they can see an easy solution.

■ Go for a walk or swim; exercise causes your body to produce endorphins, the so-called happy hormones.

■ Go to the cinema or theatre, or get engrossed in a good book.

■ Listen to some music or watch an absorbing television programme or video.

■ Soak in a warm bubble bath; a warm bath before bed raises the body temperature and may help you to sleep, which is particularly useful if you are lying awake at night worrying.

■ Have a warm shower and visualize the stress running out of you.

■ Meditate, practise yoga or do a relaxation exercise (see right).

■ Go for a massage, ask your spouse to give you a massage, or try self massage (see p. 59).

■ Buy an audio or video tape teaching relaxation techniques.

■ Don't fill up on "junk" or sugary food in place of a well-balanced diet. This may give you a temporary lift, but can leave you deficient in nutrients and can add to your stress.

■ Resist the temptation to turn to a cigarette or to alcohol to relieve your stress.

BREATHING AND RELAXATION

The natural reaction to tension or anxiety is to alter our normal breathing pattern, to take rapid, shallow and irregular breaths into the upper part of the chest. This is known as hyperventilation and can cause dizziness and aggravate feelings of anxiety. If it happens in labour, it can also increase any feelings of panic or of being out of control which, in turn, may make it more difficult to cope with contractions in labour and may make labour more painful. Smooth, easy breathing can, on the other hand, help release tension and bring on a state of relaxation. Breathing techniques form an integral part of most antenatal classes.

PRACTISING RELAXATION

I Wear loose comfortable clothing, choose a warm quiet room and unplug the phone. Sit comfortably or lie down on a carpet or blanket with your head and neck supported, your legs bent and feet apart (Do not lie flat on your back to relax during the late stages of pregnancy as the baby may press against one of the major blood vessels, restricting blood flow across the placenta and making you feel faint or dizzy.)

2 Unclench your hands so that your fingers curl naturally. Drop your shoulders and relax your jaw. Close your eyes and try to empty your mind of thoughts or visualize a peaceful place. Starting with your toes, tense and relax every part of your body, until your whole body feels limp and heavy.

3 With your lips closed, take a slow, deep breath in through your nose, filling your lungs with air so that you feel your stomach muscles rise. Breathe out gently through your lips in a blowing, sighing motion. Continue until you feel completely relaxed. Try not to let any thoughts arise.

3

4 Consciously concentrate on the rhythm of your breathing, feeling the air flowing into and out of your lungs. Check every so often that your whole body is still relaxed, and if not, tense and relax any areas that are not. When you feel ready to get up, support yourself on your hands and your left knee.

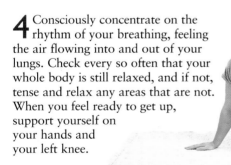

5 Place your left foot flat on the floor and push up with your hands. This is also an ideal way to end a more formal exercise session, or to restore flagging energy levels, perhaps after a day at work, but it takes practise to be able to switch off completely.

REMINDERS

Being under pressure while you are pregnant is bad for you and your baby. Start now to learn strategies to cope when you are feeling stressed. Moderate, regular exercise will make it easier to cope with minor discomforts, help you to sleep and increase the healthy glow of pregnancy that most women experience, usually in the second trimester.

■ Use simple switching-off strategies.

■ Don't lie flat on your back after the fourth or fifth month of pregnancy.

■ Learn breathing and relaxation exercises.

■ Certain aromatherapy oils are not suitable for pregnant women and should not be used without consulting a trained aromatherapist.

■ Check with your doctor before doing exercise if you have been ill, have had a miscarriage or have a complicated pregnancy.

■ When exercising, be aware of your breathing and never hold your breath.

■ Always follow the exercise guidelines, listen to what your body is telling you, and don't push yourself.

■ Exercise should be enjoyable, not a penance. Even simple and moderate exercise, such as half an hour's brisk walking a day, is beneficial.

■ Make sure that a trained instructor takes your exercise or relaxation class and always inform the instructor that you are pregnant.

■ The recommended duration of aerobic exercise is less than 45 minutes, with strenuous exercise not more than 15 minutes.

■ Stop exercising and consult your doctor if you experience any of the following symptoms:

Vaginal bleeding
A leak or gush of amniotic fluid
Pain of any kind
Contractions or abdominal pain
Nausea, dizziness or faintness
Shortness of breath
Palpitations or very rapid heart beat
Any swelling or numbness
Pain in the legs or difficulty in walking
Persistent headaches
Visual disturbances
Decreased foetal movements
Excessive tiredness

Antenatal Care, Labour and Birth

4

ANTENATAL CARE, LABOUR AND BIRTH

While you are pregnant you will probably receive more medical care and attention than at any other stage of your life. You will be asked to attend regular antenatal checks to chart your baby's growth and development. Several routine procedures will be carried out to confirm that all is well with you, too. If there are complications with your pregnancy or if it falls into the high-risk category, you may be offered more specific tests and be seen more frequently by health-care professionals. If you are not sure what a test is for or whether it is necessary, discuss it further with your doctor or midwife.

Your antental care, however, is also about preparation for labour and birth. Most births are straighforward, but intervention sometimes becomes necessary. A part of good care is to prepare you to cope with every eventuality in the labour room and to understand what is happening at each stage. Some parents-to-be and their carers formalize all these discussions by making a birth plan.

4

CHECKS FOR YOU

During pregnancy your health will be monitored regularly. You will probably be asked to attend monthly check-ups until 28 to 32 weeks, then every two weeks until 36 weeks, then weekly until delivery. A number of tests may be carried out to make sure that everything is all right. Some of these are routine, others may be special tests offered if problems occur or you are considered to be at risk, if you are over 35 or have a family history of medical conditions that could affect your pregnancy, for example (see pp. 68–69). If there is anything that you don't understand, don't be afraid to ask the midwife or doctor to explain. Use the Personal File (pp. 104–105) to jot down questions and to keep your own pregnancy record.

BLOOD TESTS

BLOOD GROUP AND RHESUS (RH) FACTOR
A blood sample will be taken to test for your blood group in case a transfusion is needed later and for your rhesus (Rh) factor. If you are Rh negative, and your baby Rh positive, you will be given medication to prevent your body producing antibodies that fight your baby's blood.

RUBELLA IMMUNITY
Your doctor will check if you are immune to rubella (German measles), which can be dangerous in the first three months of pregnancy (see p. 8).

HAEMOGLOBIN LEVELS
Your blood will be checked for levels of haemoglobin (red blood cells) to check whether you are anaemic. If levels are very low, iron may be prescribed.

DISEASES AND DISORDERS
Hepatitis B, HIV virus and syphilis can be indicated by a blood test. Genetic disorders such as sickle cell anaemia and thalassaemia (see p. 9) will be tested for if you are at risk of being a carrier.

GLUCOSE TOLERANCE
Some doctors ask their patients to take a high glucose drink at approximately 28 weeks to test for "gestational" diabetes. If a blood sample reveals an abnormally high level of glucose, you may be treated as diabetic while you are pregnant.

YOUR FIRST ANTENATAL VISIT

You will probably have your first and longest antenatal check between 8 and 12 weeks of pregnancy when your midwife or doctor will take down a detailed family history. You may be given your notes to keep, or you may be given a record card containing an abbreviated form of them. Take this with you whenever you attend clinic, or if you go away from home in case you need medical attention in an emergency.

In addition to the tests carried out at every visit, you will be given a physical examination and an internal examination.

PHYSICAL EXAMINATION

Your doctor will check your heart, lungs, and breasts, and make sure your general health is good. Your height will also be checked – if you are small, you may have a small pelvis which may make a vaginal delivery more difficult and the possibility of a caesarean birth may be discussed.

INTERNAL EXAMINATION

Your doctor may do this to confirm your pregnancy and the size of your uterus. Alternatively, you may be offered an early ultrasound scan (see pp. 68–69). A cervical smear may also be carried out to check for any cell abnormalities or infection, and a swab test may be done to check for sexually transmitted diseases (STD). If you are at risk of having an STD, ask what is being looked for.

AT EVERY VISIT

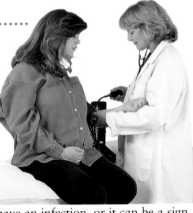

BLOOD PRESSURE

This will be monitored to check that it is within normal range. If it rises significantly, it can be a warning sign of high blood pressure. You will be advised to rest and your doctor will monitor you closely.

URINE

This will be tested for sugar and protein. Consistently high levels of sugar may indicate diabetes (many women develop diabetes in pregnancy; it disappears after the birth). Traces of protein may mean you have an infection, or it can be a sign of pre-eclampsia (very high blood pressure).

WEIGHT

This may be monitored at every visit (not all doctors do this). A gain of between 10–16.5 kg (22–35 lb) is normal but a sudden large weight gain can indicate pre-eclampsia or diabetes.

PALPATION

Your abdomen will be felt so that the size and position of your baby can be checked. The foetal heartbeat is checked as soon as it is audible.

HOW BABIES DEVELOP

Doctors date pregnancy from your last menstrual period, so that about two weeks after conception, you are termed "four weeks pregnant"; the average pregnancy lasts about 40 weeks, although a baby born after 37 weeks is considered "term". Up to eight weeks, the developing baby is called an embryo, and from then on, a foetus. Even in the womb babies develop at different rates, but if your baby seems to have stopped growing, your doctor will check what is the reason. Most first-time mothers do not recognize their babies' earliest movements (second-time mothers are more sure). If you do not feel your baby move by about week 20, or your baby has started to move and then seems to stop, contact your midwife or doctor for further advice. The chances are that a quiet spell means that your baby is asleep, but it always worth checking if you are concerned.

4

4-6 weeks
Your baby will have buried itself into the lining of your uterus by the fourth week of pregnancy and is the size of a pinhead. At 6 weeks, the baby is about 6mm ('⁄₄ in) long and the head, body and "limb buds" are formed.

8–10 weeks
Your baby's heart is now beating 140 to 150 times a minute and can be picked up on ultrasound. She has grown to 13–25mm (½ –1 in) long, and her major organs (heart, lungs, liver and kidneys) are almost formed. Her eyes, ears, fingers and toes are in their correct position and nearly formed.

11–12 weeks
Your baby's most vulnerable stage is almost over, since most of her major organs, including the sex organs, are formed. But it is still impossible to tell the baby's gender on an ultrasound scan. Her head is becoming more rounded, and her kidneys have started to function. She is now about 75mm (3 in) long.

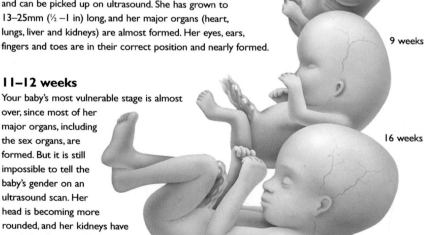

6 weeks

8 weeks

9 weeks

16 weeks

15–16 weeks

By 16 weeks your baby has developed fingers and toes, can make facial expressions, suck her fingers and drink in some of the amniotic fluid and pass it out through the bladder. A fine hair called lanugo covers the whole body. She now weighs about 125g (4 oz). You may even feel the first "butterfly" type movements from your baby. The time a women first becomes aware of her baby's movements is often called "quickening".

18–20 weeks

At around this time, most mothers can definitely feel their baby kicking or moving. You may even be able to see these movements under your skin. She has hair on her head and her eyebrows and eyelashes have developed. The skin is covered with a white greasy substance called vernix. This protects your baby from the amniotic fluid. Ask your doctor or midwife to check if you have not felt your baby move by 20 weeks.

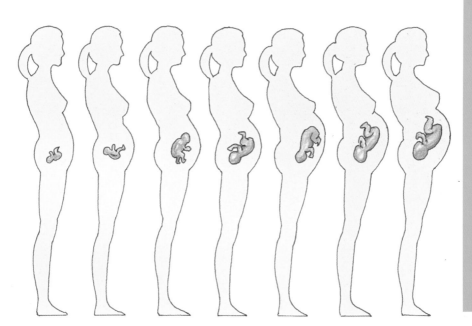

4

24 weeks

Your baby's skin has started to thicken. She can hear more clearly and loud sudden noises may make her jump. Her eyes are open and she has periods of waking and sleeping. Babies born after 24 weeks have a chance of surviving with intensive care. She now weighs about 600g (1¼ lb) and is about 36cm (14 in) long.

32 weeks

Her lungs are now mature enough for her to breathe on her own, and if born, she has a very good chance of surviving. She weighs about 1.3kg (3 lb) and is about 40cm (16 in) long.

36–40 weeks

All organs are now fully formed and working normally. At any time from 36 weeks, her head may "engage", or move down into the pelvis. She is now ready to be born.

TESTS FOR YOUR BABY

In addition to the routine tests and check-ups discussed on pages 64–65, some special screening tests may also be carried out to identify a wide range of foetal abnormalities. Not all these tests are available in every hospital and some may be offered only if your baby is thought to be at a high risk from a particular condition. Although most of the tests are perfectly safe, some do carry a small risk of a miscarriage, so you will need to weigh this, and the possible implications of the results of the tests, up before you agree to a test.

Tests can be divided into screening tests which will indicate the risk to you of having a baby with an abnormality, and diagnostic tests which will tell you whether or not your baby is affected by an abnormality. Most women who have a screening test go on to have normal babies.

ULTRASOUND

An ultrasound scan involves placing a probe over your abdomen. Sound waves sent to the uterus are then reflected back, allowing a moving picture of the foetus to be reflected on the screen. Scans measure the size of the foetus and identify some physical signs of abnormalities. (It may also be possible to see the genitals, thereby determining the baby's sex; if you don't want to know, say so.) A scan is usually carried out routinely around 18–20 weeks, but may be done earlier to diagnose pregnancy.

Most parents-to-be find their ultrasound scans one of the most thrilling parts of pregnancy as they see their baby moving around in the womb. In some cases you may be offered a photograph of the image; in others a video may be available. If you want one, you may have to ask for it.

4

SELECTIVE TESTS

Alphafetoprotein (AFP)

Here the levels of Alphafetoprotein (AFP), a substance produced by the foetus, are measured in the mother's bloodstream, normally between 15–18 weeks of pregnancy. Higher levels than expected could indicate the pregnancy is more advanced than was thought, may be caused by twins, or may occur if the baby has a neural tube defect, such as spina bifida. Lower levels than expected could indicate the pregnancy is less advanced than believed or Down's syndrome. Follow-up tests will be carried out if necessary.

■ You may be offered further special tests (if available) if your AFP levels seem too high or low, if you are over the age of 35, or if there are other risk factors in your pregnancy. Before having any further diagnostic tests, the implications of them should be explained and you should receive counselling from your doctor or midwife. You are entitled to refuse any tests offered. Current diagnostic tests include:

Chorionic Villus Sampling

■ Involves removing a small sample of cells from the placenta. Carries a higher risk of miscarriage than amniocentesis.

■ This test is usually carried out to detect some serious foetal disorders such as cystic fibrosis, Down's Syndrome, Tay-Sach's and sickle cell anaemia; but not for spina bifida.

Amniocentesis

■ A sample of amniotic fluid (which has the same genetic make-up as the baby) is withdrawn through the abdomen with a fine needle. Carries a slight risk of miscarriage.

■ The procedure is performed during the 14–18th week of pregnancy. It may be offered when the woman is over 35 or when the family history suggests there may be a risk of foetal abnormalities, chromosomal abnormalities or genetic disorders.

Triple test

■ This blood test is an extension of the AFP test and is more accurate.

■ There is also a new quadruple test which may be offered in some centres, to detect Down's syndrome.

■ The triple test is ideally carried out at 16–18 weeks to detect the risk of Down's and other chromosomal abnormalities.

Cordocentesis (umbilical vein sampling)

■ This examines the blood of the foetus from the umbilical cord. The risk of miscarriage is between 1 and 4 per 100, depending on the unit.

■ Cordocentisis can be carried out from the 18th week of pregnancy to test for infections in the foetus such as rubella or toxoplasmosis or if an amniocentesis result is unclear. It can also be used to check for metabolic disorders.

4

MAKING A BIRTH PLAN

There are several ways to approach labour and delivery. A birth plan is a written list of your ideal preferences and priorities. This is best completed a month to six weeks before your estimated delivery date as this gives you a chance to attend antenatal classes and discuss various issues with your doctor or midwife. It is also early enough to negotiate any changes you would like to your caregiver's normal practice. Make sure your birth plan is easy to read and follow (some midwives or doctors provide special forms) and date and sign it. One copy of the plan should be clipped to your notes and another kept by you. Be prepared to be flexible if your needs change or if you or your baby's health could be compromised by sticking to your plan. Your partner or birth companion should be aware of your wishes on your birth plan and help ensure they are carried out. Different things are important to different people, so think through your priorities carefully.

If your partner is not going to be present at the birth, it is best to choose someone who you can rely on, is calm in a crisis, will give you good emotional support and will not be squeamish at the birth.

4

BIRTH COMPANION

■ Do you wish to have a birth companion, such as a partner, friend or relative, with you? If so, can you bring the companion of your choice?

■ Can he or she stay with you throughout labour and delivery, including a caesarean section if necessary?

■ Is more than one companion allowed?

Example heading:
Birth companion

I would like my sister with me during birth, as well as my partner

DURING LABOUR

■ Do you want to walk around freely during labour or would you prefer to be monitored electronically?

■ What kind of pain relief do you want, if any? If you do not want any pain relief, be sure to write this on your plan.

■ Are epidurals available?

■ Is there a TENS machine available or should you hire one?

■ Can you bring in an alternative practitioner such as an acupuncturist?

Example heading:
Pain relief

I would like to use a TENS machine and have an epidural if necessary

INDUCTION

- What are your views on induction (starting labour artificially)?
- Ask what are the usual circumstances for this?
- What methods are usually used?
- Can you opt out if you prefer to manage without help?

Example heading:
Acceleration

I do not want my membranes artificially ruptured

SPECIAL EQUIPMENT

- Do you want special equipment such as a birthing pool or a birthing chair?
- If so, will these be available?
- If you would like to have music or aromatherapy essences in the birthing room, can you bring these?

Example heading:
Music

I find music relaxing and wish to bring my own tapes

DURING THE BIRTH

- Do you mind having an episiotomy if necessary, or would you prefer to tear naturally?
- Do you want your baby delivered straight on to your stomach, or washed first?

Example heading:
Episiotomy

I would prefer an episiotomy to tearing

AFTER THE BIRTH

- Do you want a hormone injection to help deliver the placenta quickly or would you prefer it was delivered naturally?
- If you plan to breastfeed, will the baby be put straight to your breast?
- How soon do you wish to go home if you have the choice?

Example heading:
Discharge

I wish to spend only one night in hospital if all is well

4

CAESAREAN SECTION

- Can I have a choice of a general anaesthetic or an epidural?
- Can my partner stay during the operation if he wishes to?
- If my baby is well enough, can I hold her immediately after birth, or can my partner hold her while I recover?

Example heading:
Caesarean section

If I need a caesarean I would prefer an epidural and would like my partner to stay

SIGNS OF LABOUR

Only five percent of babies are born on the expected date of delivery (EDD). Most women go into labour within two weeks of this date, but it is a good idea to have your hospital bags packed from 36 weeks (see pp.106-107). Although as many babies are born after 40 weeks as before, you may find yourself very tired of waiting once your EDD has come and gone. Your doctor will continue to monitor your baby's health and, if there are no signs that labour is about to start by around 42 weeks, will probably suggest that labour is induced (started artificially).

LIGHTENING AND ENGAGEMENT

Some time during the last four weeks before birth, your baby's head will probably descend into the pelvic cavity ready for delivery. The head is then said to be "engaged". You may notice when this has happened because you will feel less pressure on your chest and upper abdomen and be able to breathe more freely again. This is known as "lightening". In second or subsequent pregnancies, the head may not engage until shortly before labour starts, or even after the membranes have ruptured.

You will feel less pressure on your diaphragm.

About 5 percent of babies do not move into this position and are born with their feet or buttocks first (in a breech position). Some breech babies are delivered vaginally; others by Caesarean.

The head is engaged, well down in the pelvic cavity.

4

CONTRACTIONS

Sometime after the 20th week of pregnancy you will experience painless tightenings of the uterus. These are known as Braxton Hicks contractions and are thought to help prepare the uterus for labour. They may become stronger and painful near your date of delivery, and may be mistaken for labour pains. True labour contractions, however, increase in intensity and frequency.

You will feel the contractions of early labour as a mild backache or as something like period pains or an aching feeling. You may also be nauseous, actually vomit, or have a bout of diarrhoea.

WHAT TO DO

Time your contractions. Once they start coming every 10—15 minutes, call your doctor, midwife or hospital. At first, contractions may be irregular, but will gradually become stronger and more frequent.

START OF LABOUR

In additon to contractions, there are two easy-to-recognize signs that mark the start of labour. These occur in any order, and may succeed each other quickly or there may be a few days between them.

■ The "show".
The plug of mucus that has helped to seal the entrance to the uterus during pregnancy comes away. Known as the "show" this is a sticky pinkish discharge, but there should not be a lot of blood.

WHAT TO DO
If you are losing blood, call your doctor or hospital immediately. Otherwise, wait for contractions to start or your waters to break.

■ The waters breaking (rupture of membranes).
The bag of amniotic fluid that surrounded your baby during pregnancy breaks, and the water comes out in a gush or a trickle, depending on the size of the tear and the position of the baby's head.

WHAT TO DO
If this happens, phone the hospital, or your midwife or doctor. You will probably be advised to go to hospital at once, even if there are no contractions, as your baby is no longer protected against infection.

WHEN SHOULD I GO TO HOSPITAL?

When to go into hospital depends on what you have been advised by your doctor or midwife, how far you live from the hospital, and how anxious you are. But a first labour may take quite a long time and you will probably feel more relaxed if you stay at home for the first few hours. In early labour, try to keep moving around and have something light to eat and drink to keep your strength up. Practise your relaxation techniques, time your contractions every so often and – if your membranes have not ruptured – have a warm bath.

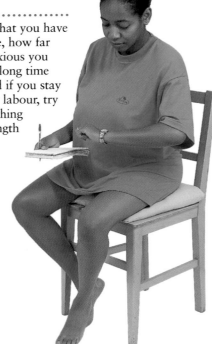

4

Warning!
If any of the above signs of labour occur before you are 36 weeks pregnant, call your hospital or doctor immediately. If labour is very premature, treatment may be given to try to stop it.

THE FIRST STAGE

There are three stages of labour which, for the birth of a first baby, lasts on average 12 to 14 hours. The first stage is the longest and from the start of established labour usually lasts 6 to 10 hours. During this time, contractions become progressively stronger and gradually open the cervix (this is called dilatation and is measured in centimetres) and pull it up and over the baby's head (effacement, measured in percentages) until it is fully open, to allow the baby to descend the birth canal.

AT THE HOSPITAL

Once you arrive at the hospital your midwife or doctor will:
- Ask you about the start of your labour
- Check your pulse, temperature, blood pressure and urine
- Examine your cervix to check how far it has dilated.

MONITORING YOUR BABY'S HEART RATE

Throughout labour your baby's heart rate will be monitored. It is usual for a baby's heart rate to dip as your contraction reaches its peak intensity, then to pick up as the contraction subsides. But any change from this pattern could indicate that your baby is not coping well with labour (this is termed "in distress"). If the baby is distressed, action may be needed to speed delivery. Monitoring may be done by:

INTERMITTENT AUSCULTATION (IA)

Here a special stethoscope called a "Pinard" or a handheld ultrasound machine called a "Doppler" is used every 15–30 minutes throughout labour and more often during the second stage. With this method you can move about freely.

ELECTRONIC FOETAL MONITORING (EFM)

The foetal heart rate is measured for 10–30 minutes every two to four hours or continuously throughout labour by a monitor strapped by a belt to your abdomen, or an electrode attached to your baby's scalp. You cannot easily move around with this method, unless your hospital uses a remote control system called telemetry. A TENS machine for pain relief (see pp. 76–77) may prevent an EFM from working properly. If you are considering a water birth, you should know that the EFM cannot be used in water.

COPING DURING LABOUR

There are no hard and fast rules about what position to adopt during labour, the main thing is that you are as relaxed and comfortable as possible. You may wish to squat, sit, kneel, lie down or use a mixture of positions. But unless you have to stay in bed for medical reasons, being upright – walking around, standing, sitting, squatting or kneeling – is less painful and may shorten labour.

SITTING

There is no way of knowing how long labour will last, so conserving your strength makes sense. Sit between contractions to rest. Lean forward to keep up pressure on the cervix, and relieve pressure on your lower back.

If you need extra support during a contraction, lean against the back of a chair. Place a pillow on the back to rest your head between contractions.

KNEELING

Kneeling as you lean forward on your arms takes pressure off the cervix. This may slow labour, but can be useful when contractions start to come close together. It also relieves pressure on your back, which can be painful.

STANDING

Early in labour standing and walking around between contractions keeps the pressure on your cervix, helping the contractions to dilate it. Lean against a wall or your birth partner for support during a contraction. Your partner can also massage your back in this position.

4

PAIN RELIEF IN LABOUR

There are different forms of pain relief available should you need it. Knowing what is available will help you to make the best choice for you and your baby. Relaxation techniques can also help you manage the pain during labour.

SELF HELP

■ Practise the breathing and relaxation techniques you learned in your antenatal class.

■ Don't hold your breath during a contraction but "breathe" through the pain by keeping your shoulders and jaw loose, and breathing out. Try not to tense as a contraction peaks – tension leads to pain.

■ Think positively when having a contraction – remind yourself that each one is bringing the birth of your baby nearer.

■ Listen to your body and adopt the position most comfortable for you.

■ If your back aches, try applying a hot water bottle or heat pad.

■ Don't be embarrassed by making noises such as grunting to help you cope.

■ Ask your partner to give you a massage, perhaps using an aromatherapy oil.

■ Create a relaxed atmosphere by burning an aromatherapy oil such as lavender, lighting a scented candle, playing music or asking for the lights to be dimmed.

DRUG RELIEF

Check with your hospital or birth centre which types of drug relief are available to you during labour.

ENTONOX (GAS AND AIR)

This is a mixture of 50% nitrous oxide and 50% oxygen which is breathed in through a mouthpiece or mask which you hold yourself, as soon as you feel the contractions start. It can help you relax, but some mothers find it makes them feel sick or "woozy", rather than taking the edge off the pain.

EPIDURAL

This is an anaesthetic injected between two spinal vertebrae in the lower back (see right), which numbs the nerves. It removes pain and can be used for an elective caesarean. In some women it lowers the blood pressure, may affect their legs and bladder for a while and may cause headaches afterward.

PETHIDINE

This is given by injection and has a calming effect. It may be combined with other drugs to relieve nausea. If given too near the second stage, it may make it harder for you to push effectively, and can make your baby sleepy or depress her breathing. Pethidine does not alter the pain, it alters your perception of it.

DRUG-FREE PAIN RELIEF

Some women find using alternative therapies such as acupuncture, hypnosis or homeopathy helpful during labour. If you want to use an alternative therapy, discuss it with your doctor or midwife and let the hospital know beforehand. Check that any practitioner is qualified and has experience with women in labour.

ACUPUNCTURE

This involves the insertion of fine needles into selected points under the skin in order to stimulate the flow of your own energy and relieve pain.

HYPNOSIS

This uses the power of the mind to induce a state of deep relaxation to relieve pain in labour, but training needs to be started weeks in advance.

HOMEOPATHY

Natural remedies are used to treat a person as a whole. Arnica is said to be particularly useful in reducing bleeding and bruising following labour. Check with a homeopath which remedies are best for labour.

TENS

Transcutaneous Electrical Nerve Stimulation (TENS) involves the use of electrodes, which are attached to the lower back. These stimulate nerve endings in the skin to trigger the release of the body's own pain relieving substances. They also prevent pain signals travelling to the brain. For some women TENS can be very effective, and it allows you to be in control. But it needs to be started early in labour for full benefit. If your hospital does not have a TENS machine, you may be able to hire one. (It's worth doing this in advance to practise with it.)

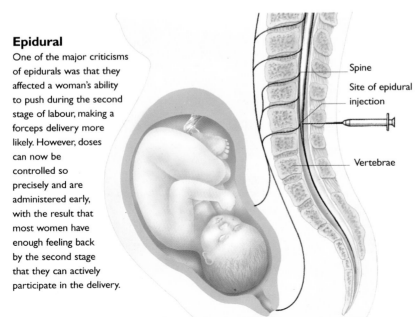

Epidural

One of the major criticisms of epidurals was that they affected a woman's ability to push during the second stage of labour, making a forceps delivery more likely. However, doses can now be controlled so precisely and are administered early, with the result that most women have enough feeling back by the second stage that they can actively participate in the delivery.

Spine

Site of epidural injection

Vertebrae

4

THE SECOND STAGE

The second stage begins when your cervix is fully dilated (at 10cm/4in) and ends when your baby is born. It lasts an average of 30 minutes to an hour, but may take as little as 10 minutes, or as much as two hours. Most doctors intervene if it goes on for longer than two hours.

TRANSITION

This is the stage between the end of the first stage and the beginning of the second, and is the most exhausting and challenging period of labour. It may be very brief or last for an hour or more. Your cervix is almost fully dilated and contractions are very strong, long and frequent.

■ During this time you may feel hot and sweaty or cold and shivery, or alternate between the two. Your legs may feel cold and tremble and you may feel nauseous or even vomit. Tell your partner what you need – socks, chipped ice to suck, a warm blanket, a cool sponge.

■ You are likely to feel a powerful urge to push or bear down. Unless you have been told to push by your doctor or midwife, it is important not to. Pushing before the cervix is fully dilated can cause it to become swollen, making it more difficult for the baby to pass through the opening. It will also bruise the cervix, which can be painful.

■ To prevent yourself from bearing down, kneel with your buttocks in the air. This takes the pressure of the baby's head off your cervix, which reduces the urge to push a little. It also helps you to conserve your energy for the hard work of the second stage.

WHAT YOUR BIRTH COMPANION CAN DO

■ Encourage you and remind you to take one contraction at a time.

■ Help you to focus on how far you have come, and how many contractions are behind you.

■ Check your needs and only talk or touch if this helps; mood swings are normal, especially during transition, and your needs will change from moment to moment.

■ Mop your brow with a cool damp cloth, if this helps.

■ Once you are given the okay to push, help your efforts to concentrate. Pushing only assists a contraction, pushing between them wastes your efforts.

■ Be there for you: you are likely to push him away at least once; he should take it all with good grace.

POSITIONS FOR THE SECOND STAGE

Once your cervix is fully dilated, you can adopt the position you find most comfortable and effective for pushing and delivery. It is much easier if you can adopt an upright position because gravity makes it easier for your baby to pass down the birth canal.

KNEELING

Kneeling is almost as good for widening the pelvis. You can hang onto your partner's neck, or your partner and the midwife can support you under your arms.

SUPPORTED SQUAT

Squatting is one of the best ways to widen the pelvis and allow gravity to push your baby out. Your partner can kneel behind you to support you under the arms, or sit behind you. You could also try a semi-squat, standing with your knees bent, while your partner supports you.

STANDARD DELIVERY POSITION

This is one of the most common delivery positions. You sit in a semi-upright position with your back supported, either on cushions or with your partner sitting behind you. Your knees should be drawn up with your legs wide apart and your hands against the back of your thighs. In this position you can hold a mirror to your vagina to see the baby's head as it emerges.

BIRTH

The nine months of waiting are now almost over, and you will soon meet your baby. If you are having a "normal delivery", your baby will be born head first without any extra help. Sometimes, however, a cesarean or other type of delivery may become necessary.

PUSHING DURING THE SECOND STAGE

To push your baby out, breathe deeply while your contraction is building up, then as it reaches a peak, push for about five seconds, or until you want to take a breath (holding your breath unnecessarily can exhaust you and may reduce the oxygen content in your baby's blood.) If the contraction is still peaking, take a few deep breaths and push again. You will probably have the urge to push three to five times in each contraction. As you push, your baby's head will become visible at each contraction, and then slip back a little in between. You may be given an episiotomy – a small cut into the perineum, the skin between the vagina and rectum, to prevent tearing of the tissue. If you do not want an episiotomy, then you can state this on your birth plan.

THE MOMENT OF BIRTH

When your baby is about to be born, her head will appear at the vaginal opening and no longer slip back – this is known as "crowning" (the skin of your perineum "crowns" her head). You may then be asked not to push, but to pant instead, as your baby's head is gently guided out. At this stage you may wish to use a mirror to see the birth, or your partner may wish to video it. Suction may be applied to your baby's mouth and nose to remove excess mucus. Another push may be needed for the shoulders and rest of the body to glide out. If your baby is not breathing, further suction or oxygen may be required. But if everything is normal, your baby may be put on your stomach while the umbilical cord is being cut, or you may be able to hold your baby immediately.

4

The head crowns and is clearly visible to your carers.

With one more contraction the head emerges.

ASSISTED DELIVERY

If your second stage is particularly difficult or prolonged, the doctor may remove the baby with the aid of forceps or a ventouse, once the head is visible. With forceps, after a local anaesthetic is given, two metal blades that look like tongs are inserted into the vagina, one at a time. These cradle the head, and the baby is drawn from the birth canal. With a ventouse, a plastic cup is attached to the head and suction applied to suck the baby out. An episiotomy is common if either method is used, however, their use may avoid the need for a caesarean section.

CAESAREAN BIRTH

About one in eight British babies and one in four American babies are born by caesarean section. Sometimes a caesarean may be planned in advance if your doctor considers it necessary (an elective caesarean), or it may become necessary as labour proceeds. The reasons for a caesarean include:

- Your baby needs delivering quickly, if for example, there is foetal distress, you have had a haemorrhage, or if you have a medical condition such as pre-eclampsia or diabetes.

- Your baby is awkwardly positioned, such as a breech or transverse (shoulder first) position.

- Your baby is large and her head is stuck in the pelvis, which is too narrow.

- Your labour is not progressing for some reason.

- The placenta is lying across the cervix.

- You are having more than one baby.

- You have active genital herpes which could infect the baby during a vaginal birth.

THE PROCEDURE

Before the operation your pubic hair will be shaved, a catheter inserted in your bladder and an intravenous infusion started in case you need medication during the delivery. You may be given a choice of a general anaesthetic, when you will be unconscious, or an epidural or spinal block, when you will be awake during the delivery but the lower part of your body will be numb. In an emergency, a general anaesthetic may be needed for speed.

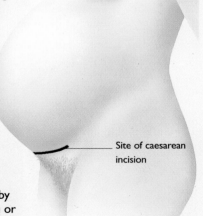

Site of caesarean incision

An incision will be made in your lower abdomen and uterus and your baby will be removed manually or with forceps. Your baby will be checked over and then given to you or your partner to hold while you are stitched.

4

THE THIRD STAGE

The third stage of labour is the shortest. It consists of expelling the placenta or afterbirth from the lining of your uterus once your baby has been born, and usually lasts from around five minutes to about half an hour. During this time you will continue to have contractions, although in the excitement of getting to know your baby you may not feel them.

DELIVERY OF THE PLACENTA

As your baby is being born you will probably be given a routine injection of a hormone preparation called oxytocin. (Proponents of natural childbirth argue against the routine use of oxytocin; oxytocin is produced by your body in response to your baby's sucking at your breast, which may render synthetic oxytocin unnecessary.) Oxytocin helps the uterus to contract and expel the placenta. Once the placenta has detached itself from the uterus, the doctor or midwife may gently pull on the cord to remove the placenta and ask you to help by pushing or bearing down. After the placenta is removed, it will be examined to make sure that it is intact and that no fragments are left inside, which can cause unnecessary bleeding and infection.

Your perineum will then be stitched if you have had a tear or an episiotomy. Your temperature, pulse, blood pressure, uterus and lochia (vaginal bleeding) will be checked and you will be made comfortable. Then you will be left with your baby and partner or birth companion.

4

TECHNICAL TERMS

- **Active birth** – an approach to childbirth that involves moving around and changing positions throughout labour. Delivery is conducted in an "upright" position after learning stretching exercises.
- **Albumin** – a protein present in tissues which is checked for in urine tests. If present it can be a sign of pre-eclampsia.
- **Amniotic fluid** –the fluid surrounding the foetus in the uterus.
- **Amniotic sac** – the layer of membranes surrounding the foetus in the uterus.
- **Apgar score** – a system used after birth to assess a baby's wellbeing.
- **Bearing down** – pushing movement made during the second stage of labour.
- **Breech presentation** – the buttocks or feet of the baby are facing downward, instead of the head.
- **Contractions** – regular tightening of uterine muscles to open the cervix to deliver the baby.
- **Crowning** – the time when the baby's head appears in the vagina and does not slip back again.
- **Dilatation** – the progressive opening of the cervix in response to uterine contractions.
- **EDD** – expected date of delivery.
- **Embryo** – name for the developing baby up to eight weeks of pregnancy.
- **Engaged** – when the baby's head has settled into the pelvic cavity.
- **Foetal distress** – occurs when there is a shortage of oxygen reaching the foetus.
- **Foetus** – name for the developing baby after the eighth week of pregnancy.
- **Fontanelles** – two soft spots on the baby's head where the bones have not yet joined.
- **Gestation** – the length of time between conception and birth.
- **Haemorrhage** – heavy bleeding. (Antepartum haemorrhage is bleeding before the baby is born, postpartum haemorrhage is bleeding after the baby is born.)
- **Induction** – artificial starting of labour.
- **Lie** – the position of the baby in the uterus.
- **Lightening** – relief from abdominal pressure that follows the engagement of the baby's head.
- **Moulding** – the shaping of the baby's skull as it passes through the vagina.
- **Pelvic floor** – the "hammock" of muscles that supports the bladder, lower bowel and uterus.
- **Perineum** – the area of skin between the vagina and rectum.
- **Placenta** – the organ that provides oxygen and nutrients for the foetus and carries its waste products to the mother's system.
- **Pre-eclampsia** – a potentially dangerous condition characterised by high blood pressure, swelling of the hands, face and feet, sudden and excessive weight gain, and albumin in the urine.
- **Quickening** – first foetal moments felt by the mother.
- **Uterus (Womb)** – the organ in the body in which the baby develops.

4

REMINDERS

In the excitement of your pregnancy, as you watch your shape change to accommodate your growing baby, some things may slip your mind. This checklist will help you to remember the most important parts of your antenatal care, and serve as a quick reminder of what to do during labour and birth.

■ It is essential to keep your antenatal appointments so that any problems or complications can be detected early.

■ If there is anything that you don't understand about your antenatal care, don't be afraid to ask the midwife or doctor to explain.

■ Take your antenatal notes or record with you whenever you attend clinic, or if you go away from home, in case you need emergency medical attention.

■ The majority of special tests indicate that a baby is in good health and developing normally.

■ Some special tests carry a slight risk to the foetus. If special tests indicate that there may be foetal abnormalities, you may have to decide whether you want to continue with your pregnancy. If you are not sure what a test is for, or whether it is necessary, discuss this further with your doctor or midwife. You are entitled to refuse any test. If tests do indicate an abnormality, you will normally have time to seek counselling before making a final decision.

■ If you do not feel your baby move by 18–20 weeks or if your baby has started to move and then seems to stop, contact your midwife or doctor immediately for advice.

■ Your birth companion does not have to be your spouse, but could be a friend or relative. If you can think of no one you would like to be at the birth, tell your midwife who can arrange for one of her colleagues to support you.

■ If you have preferences for what you would like to happen in labour and delivery, complete your birth plan 4–6 weeks before your expected date of delivery. Be prepared to be flexible if your needs change or if you or your baby's health could be compromised by sticking to your plan.

■ Only 5 percent of babies are born on the expected date of delivery (EDD). Most women go into labour within two weeks either side of this date. It is a good idea to have your hospital bags packed from 36 weeks.

■ The three signs that can be recognised as the start of labour and which can occur in any order are the show, your waters breaking, and contractions.

■ Contractions that do not increase in frequency or intensity are probably not real labour contractions.

■ If your pregnancy lasts longer than about 42 weeks, or labour is prolonged or delayed, the doctor may decide to start or augment it artificially.

■ Every contraction brings you closer to seeing your baby.

■ Nothing you say or do in the labour room will shock, alarm or distress the medical staff involved in your care.

You and Your Baby

5

YOU AND YOUR BABY

Congratulations. After nine months of anticipation you are now responsible for a tiny baby 24 hours a day – it is not surprising that many parents feel a bit "shell shocked" for the first few weeks. Don't worry: in no time you will be confidently caring for your baby's needs and enjoying his presence in your lives. In the six weeks after the birth, your body will return to its pre-pregnancy state. Understanding these changes and looking after yourself is an essential part of your own wellbeing, so eat well, exercise and rest. If you are in pain or have any problems, don't suffer in silence. Tell your doctor or midwife. In these weeks your baby will change, too: you may see his first smile in this period, you will both learn how rewarding breastfeeding can be, you will start to interpret his cries and anticipate his needs. Above all, you will enjoy learning how to be a parent.

5

POSTNATAL CARE

Unless your baby was born by caesarean section, you will probably stay in hospital for one to three days, although if all is well you could go home within a few hours after birth. When you go home you need to be aware of what is normal after birth, and when you should check with your doctor or midwife. A midwife may visit you at home but you should check what is normal practice in your area.

YOUR PHYSICAL HEALTH

LOCHIA
■ This is the blood and discharge passed from the uterus following birth. It is heavy and red at first, and clots may be passed for 2–4 days. It gradually becomes pinker and lighter and after 2–3 weeks (but sometimes longer) becomes pale and brown, then ceases.

■ Use sanitary pads rather than tampons, as tampons may introduce infection.

■ Tell your doctor or midwife if the discharge smells offensive or you have a bright-red blood loss or pass clots after the first 4–5 days.

PERINEAL PAIN AND STITCHES
During delivery, the perineum (the area around the vaginal area) often becomes bruised and swollen. You may also have needed stitches. Usually the pain eases once the wound has healed, normally within 7–10 days, but this may sometimes last longer.

■ Ask your doctor for a local anaesthetic spray or oral medication for the pain.

■ Bathe the area several times a day with plain warm water. (Or sit in a plastic bowl or baby's bath.) Pat dry with a soft towel, gauze or soft toilet paper.

■ To help bruising, try arnica tablets, arnica cream (but not on an open wound) or a pad of chilled witch hazel.

■ Apply an ice pack (a bag of frozen vegetables wrapped in a clean cloth is fine).

■ Drink plenty of fluids to dilute the urine and stop it from stinging.

■ Take measures to prevent constipation (see p. 37).

■ To promote healing, do pelvic floor exercises (see p. 55).

■ Use soft, thick sanitary pads: the thinner ones are harsher.

AFTERPAINS
As your uterus returns to its normal pre-pregnancy size, you may feel contraction-like pains for the first few days.

■ Try mild analgesics such as paracetamol or ibuprofen, and relaxation breathing (see p. 60).

■ Avoid codeine, which can cause constipation.

OTHER POSTNATAL CONCERNS

■ Your periods may return within the first six weeks, but especially if you are breastfeeding, they may not return for several months.

■ Sexual intercourse is safe as soon as you and your partner are ready, but you may not feel ready for several months. Try to stay close physically even if you do not want to make love.

■ Although sex may be sore at first, it should not hurt. If it does, ask your doctor to check for any problems. Use a lubricating jelly or different positions.

■ Even if you have not had a period or are breastfeeding, if you have sex you can still get pregnant. Ask your doctor for contraceptive advice.

CAESAREAN SECTION

After a caesarean, it is normal to have abdominal pain and discomfort at first, but you should be offered adequate pain relief and extra help in caring for your baby. To help your general recovery, you will be encouraged to move around as soon as possible, and to do breathing and leg exercises (see pp. 56–57). Your wound will be checked regularly.

POSTNATAL EXERCISES

You're feeling exhausted. Your stitches are hurting. The baby's just stopped crying and you want to rest. The last thing you may feel like doing are postnatal exercises. However, gentle exercises really will help to improve circulation, give you some energy, and help get flabby muscles back into shape, which may boost your morale. Turn to pages 55–57 for a reminder about how to do these.

5

POSTNATAL CHECK

About six weeks after the birth, you should have a postnatal check by your doctor when you can discuss any problems. But if you are worried in any way, make an appointment before then. All women recover from childbirth differently, so don't take what anyone else is feeling as an indicator of your health.

POSTNATAL EMOTIONS

It is normal to feel a mixture of emotions in the first days and weeks after having a baby. You may feel "out of touch" with your body, exhausted after delivery and with meeting the demands of a new baby, and confused about your feelings for your baby and your partner. During this period, it is important that you are kind to yourself, listen to your body, and give yourself time to recover.

FEELING BLUE?

Most mothers suffer from mood swings or the "baby blues" about three to five days after birth, when they feel weepy, angry or depressed. This is thought to be due to a sudden fall in hormone levels. If the "blues" don't go away within a week or two, or get worse, talk to your doctor; you may be suffering from postnatal depression.

POSTNATAL DEPRESSION

This is an extremely distressing condition which is thought to affect at least one woman in ten. Although it usually appears within 2–8 weeks after birth, it can appear up to six months or even a year after the birth. Many women are reluctant to admit to postnatal depression, or they may deny their symptoms. However, effective treatment is available and if you feel you are suffering from postnatal depression, it is essential that you seek help.

- Signs and symptoms include:
    Crying and anxiety
    Panic attacks
    Sleeplessness
    Aches and pains
    Tiredness (all new parents are tired, but the lethargy that may accompany
        postnatal depression is different)
    Feeling unable to cope
    Indifference towards the baby or frequent concerns about the baby
    Memory loss
    Feelings of unreality
    Loss of self esteem
    Loss of appetite or excessive appetite
    Inability to concentrate
    Antagonism toward your partner.

- Treatment includes support, counselling and perhaps medication.

- Some sufferers from postnatal depression respond positively to treatment with progesterone.

- Some women may also benefit from complementary therapies such as massage, acupuncture or homeopathy, but it is important to see a qualified practitioner and to inform your GP.

5

COPING WITH TIREDNESS

Many mothers find the first few weeks of looking after a new baby a shock to the system. Constant feeding and changing, snatched meals and broken nights, plus perhaps lots of well-meaning visitors, can leave you feeling exhausted. Things really will get better as you find yourself getting used to your baby, getting into a routine and regaining your energy. To help you beat tiredness:

■ Get plenty of rest. Unplug the phone if necessary.

■ Limit visitors and make sure they entertain themselves. Put a notice on your door if you do not want to be disturbed.

■ Only do essential housework; if you can, pay for some help.

■ Don't be a martyr and feel you have to do everything yourself. Accept any help that is offered, or if necessary, ask for it.

■ Practise relaxation techniques you learned during pregnancy (see pp. 58–61).

■ Do something that makes you feel good – have a massage, haircut, or even go for a walk or swim on your own.

■ Don't neglect eating. A good, well-balanced diet is just as important now as it was in pregnancy. Try to avoid "junk fast foods" and remember, healthy snacks are nourishing and easy to prepare if you haven't yet time or appetite for cooked meals (see p. 31 for ideas).

YOU AND YOUR PARTNER

Adjusting to your new relationship as parents is not always easy. Try to spend a little time together each day to talk about your feelings and have physical contact, even if you do not make love.

WHAT FATHERS CAN DO

■ Get to know your baby. Cuddle, talk, bathe and change her. Parenthood is a shared experience.

■ Feed the baby if she is bottlefed or support your partner if she is breastfeeding.

■ Take the baby for a walk in the pram to spend time with her and give your partner a break.

■ Help as much as possible with household chores. If you cook a meal, cook double and freeze half for another day.

■ Make allowances for your partner's changing emotions but if you think she may be depressed, seek help.

5

YOUR NEW BABY

Seeing a newborn for the first time can be quite a shock. Although it is rarely a disappointment for parents, you may have mentally pictured a smooth-cheeked dream baby as portrayed in advertisements. Instead, you may have a baby who is covered with a white waxy substance, with a wrinkled red face and perhaps some other strange features that you feel concerned about. Before you start to worry, be reassured that very few babies look perfect at birth and most irregularities will disappear within a few weeks. Your baby will also be checked at birth to make sure that everything is all right.

FIRST CHECKS

Checks carried out immediately after birth by the doctor or midwife include:

■ Apgar score: this is used to assess breathing, heart rate, reflexes, skin colour and muscle tone, at one minute and five minutes after birth. The baby is given a rating of 0, 1 or 2 for each measure, which are then combined. A very low rating will merit immediate medical intervention, but a low score is not necessarily a cause for alarm. Few normal babies achieve the maximum score of 10, even after five minutes.

■ Weight, head circumference and length.

■ A "top to tail" check from head to toes, including the mouth to make sure there is no cleft palate, and the hips for any dislocation.

■ Before leaving hospital, your baby will also be given a physical examination by the doctor, including the heart and lungs, abdomen, hips and reflexes.

REFLEXES

Your baby is born with several reflex actions that are early protection measures. The strongest of these are rooting and sucking, which help her to feed (see pp. 98–99). If you put your finger in her hand, she will grasp this tightly (grasp reflex). Or if she is scared, she will fling her arms and legs wide (startle or Moro reflex). Most reflexes disappear by two to three months.

5

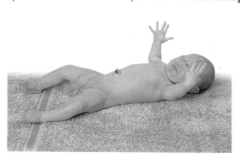

Moro, or "startle" reflex

Grasp reflex

Fontanelles

These are the "soft spots" on the top of the head where the scalp bones have not yet joined together. It is normal for them to beat. The back fontanelle closes in about 6–8 weeks and the larger front fontanelle gradually closes by 18 months.

Skin

Many babies are covered in vernix, a white greasy substance which protects the baby from the amniotic fluid in the womb. This can be washed off or left to absorb. If your baby was overdue, the skin may be dry or flaky.

Genitals

Some boys may have fluid around the testicles and girls sometimes have a white or blood-stained discharge from the vagina. Both conditions will disappear without treatment.

Eyes

The eyes may be sticky and swollen at first. See p. 96 for advice on cleaning.

Cord

The cord stump shrivels and usually falls off in about a week to ten days; your doctor or midwife will advise you on keeping it clean. Tell your doctor or midwife if there is any bleeding or discharge.

Breasts

Both sexes sometimes have swollen breasts, and there may be a milky discharge. These are due to the effects of your hormones and will disappear without treatment over a few weeks.

Head

A baby's head is large in proportion to the rest of the body. It is common for it to be misshapen and there may be a soft bump or a cystlike swelling due to pressure of the head on the dilating cervix. These are all temporary and will disappear over a few weeks.

BOWELS

The stools change over a few days from greeny/black meconium to a greenish-brown colour, then yellow colour. They are often runny in breastfed babies; bottlefed babies usually have larger, firmer stools. The number of stools passed varies. As long as they are soft and a normal colour, there is no need to worry if the bowels are not opened every day or if they are opened several times a day.

WEIGHT

It is normal for babies to lose some weight during the first few days. This is usually regained within 10–14 days.

5

BRINGING BABY HOME

Many mothers are discharged from hospital within 24 hours of giving birth, before having time to learn basic childcare skills. It can be quite frightening to start looking after your baby yourself, so before leaving hospital, try to learn as much about baby care as you can. In some countries, a midwife will call at your home for up to 10 days, followed by the health visitor, to give you further help and advice. If these services are not available to you, check whether your insurance will cover a home consultation with a visiting nurse. Although caring for your baby is a demanding, 24-hour job, it is also infinitely rewarding. And as you get to know each other and you become skilled in handling her, your confidence will grow.

THE RIDE HOME

Going home from the hospital, the baby should be securely strapped in an appropriate restrainer. It is not safe to to carry your baby on your lap. The car seat you use must comply with government safety standards and be fitted to the manufacturers instructions. Infants should use a rear-facing seat until they are about nine months old, or weigh about 10kg (22 lb). If your car has a passenger-side airbag, the baby seat must be fitted to the rear seat of the car, not the front seat.

GETTING ORGANIZED

The basic needs of a new baby are food, sleep, warmth and loving attention. Babies rarely feed and sleep to order during the first few weeks and the only way they have to express their needs is by crying. Although you will eventually get into a daily routine, expect the first few weeks to be hectic and haphazard, and decide on your priorities. It will help you enormously if you can sleep or rest when your baby does and eat in between her feeds, rather than trying to fit her into your schedule. The first few weeks do not set a pattern for the rest of her babyhood, so don't worry that she will never settle into a routine.

■ Routines should be flexible and realistic, and will change as your baby grows.

■ Don't try to keep to a timetable for feeding your baby, but let her feed on demand. This will help you to get breastfeeding well established. She will eventually get into her own routine.

■ Don't try to keep your young baby awake during the day so that she will sleep at night – she needs to sleep when she wants to. As she gets older, a routine will emerge.

5

FEELINGS FOR YOUR BABY

You may be overjoyed by the birth and already overwhelmed by love for your baby. Or you may feel very protective of this vulnerable new being, without actually feeling love. Some may have had a difficult birth and need a little time to get themselves on an even keel before they can really start to relate to their babies. If you feel detached or don't feel any love for her, don't panic or feel guilty. Although it is important that you and your baby enjoy a warm and loving relationship, many mothers and fathers do not fall in love or "bond" with their baby at first. Like other relationships, some get off to a slower start than others and need time to grow. The word "bonding" implies that love is like a glue, instantly applied and irremovable, but relationships simply are not like that. If you are worried about your feelings for your baby, talk to your doctor or midwife.

SIBLING JEALOUSY

If you have a toddler, try to prepare him as much as possible for the arrival of the baby. But even if he seems pleased and affectionate towards her, don't be surprised if he is jealous, if he regresses to an earlier stage of behaviour, or exhibits behaviours such as being demanding, clinging or defiant.

- When he meets the baby, have a present ready "from the baby". It helps if he can come to hospital to "bring her home".
- Ask visitors to make a fuss of your toddler before the baby.
- Give your toddler extra cuddles and reassurance that you love him.
- Involve him in helping with the baby as much as possible if he wants to, but if he sees it as a chore, rather than a sign of maturity, don't force it.
- Reinforce his maturity by letting him decide if he wants to go to playgroup, choose what he wants for lunch or what he would like to wear.
- Jealousy is normal.

PETS

Don't invest in a pet if you've just had a baby – looking after two newcomers can be difficult. If you already have a pet, follow the guidelines listed below to avoid passing on any infections to your baby:

- Let a vet check your pet before the baby is born. Make sure your pet has the necessary inoculations, is dewormed regularly and is free from fleas.
- If you have a dog, discourage it from licking your baby's face.
- If you have a cat, buy a net for your baby's cot and pram.
- If you know your pet is likely to be jealous of the baby, make sure the two are never left alone together.

5

BASIC BABY CARE

When picking your baby up, whether to change, bath or feed her, always hold her firmly and confidently and talk to her softly and gently, making eye contact.

PICKING UP YOUR BABY

Holding and cuddling your baby makes her feel safe and loved, but this may not come naturally at first, and you may feel nervous.

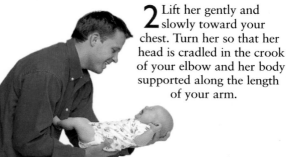

1 Standing facing her, slide one hand under her head and neck and the other beneath her lower back and bottom.

2 Lift her gently and slowly toward your chest. Turn her so that her head is cradled in the crook of your elbow and her body supported along the length of your arm.

3 When you put her down, support her head and bottom. Slide your hand out from under her bottom first, then from beneath her head.

HOLDING YOUR BABY

There are several ways that babies like to be held, but a newborn baby cannot support her head, so always support her head and neck to stop her head flopping back. Use a sling so that she is in close contact with you, but your arms are free to do other things.

5

1 Cuddle her against your shoulder with one hand supporting the back of her neck and head and the other under her bottom. Hold her upright to look over your shoulder.

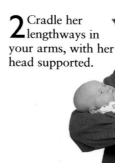

2 Cradle her lengthways in your arms, with her head supported.

PUTTING ON A VEST

Most babies dislike having clothes pulled over their head. You may prefer to buy crossover vests that tie or snap shut at the side.

1 Gather the vest at the neck with the front facing you. Place the back of the vest at your baby's crown.

2 Gently raise her head and slip the vest over her face, taking care not to drag it. Pull the vest down over her neck and shoulders and lower her down.

3 Gather up the sleeve with one hand, stretch the opening wide, and holding your baby's wrist, guide her arm through. Repeat with the other arm. Pull it down behind her back and do up the poppers under her bottom.

CHANGING YOUR BABY'S NAPPY

To help prevent nappy rash, change your baby's nappy as soon as you can when it becomes wet or soiled. As a guideline you may find that newborn babies need changing 10–12 times a day.

1 Lie your baby on a changing mat or other flat surface (try to have this at waist height so that you do not have to bend). Remove the old nappy. Lift her legs up by the ankles with one hand and use the old nappy to clean off the worst of any soiling. Roll up the old nappy and put it in a plastic bag.

2 Thoroughly clean the whole area, wiping from front to back with moist cotton wool. Wipes are harsh for a newborn but fine after a couple of months.

3 When your baby's bottom is clean and dry, wash and dry your hands and apply a barrier cream to her bottom. Lift her legs up by the ankles with one hand and slide a nappy under her with the other hand. Secure the clean nappy.

5

BASIC BABY CARE

Looking after your baby will quickly become second nature, but remember that your way will always be slightly different from anybody else's. Baby care is about finding out what works for you and your baby.

"TOPPING AND TAILING"

Your newborn baby does not need a bath every day – once every few days is fine. In between you can keep her clean by "topping and tailing". This means undressing your baby a little at a time, and only cleaning the parts that need it, such as her face, hands and bottom. Never try to clean inside her nose or ears, as her mucous membranes are self-cleaning. Just wipe away any visible wax or mucus with damp cotton wool. Use only cooled boiled water and cotton wool – soap will dry her skin and talcum powder may cause breathing problems.

1 Dip a fresh piece of cotton wool into cooled boiled water and wipe one eye from the nose outward. Repeat with a fresh piece of cotton wool for the other eye. Wipe the skin folds in the neck and under the arms. Pat dry with a soft cloth or towel.

5

2 Put her vest back on, then use warm water to wash her hands. Undo her nappy and clean her bottom. Pay particular attention to the creases at the top of her thighs. If her toes are tightly curled, gently uncurl them to wipe the soles of her feet. Pat dry with a soft cloth or towel. Let her kick without a nappy for a while, then finish dressing her.

BATHING

1 Collect everything you need before you start, including a waterproof apron, baby toiletries, cotton wool and cooled boiled water, sponge or soft flannel, clean nappy and clothes.

2 Put cold water in the bath first, followed by hot, and test the temperature with your elbow. The water should be warm but not hot.

3 Undress your baby and wrap her snugly in a soft towel across your lap. Wipe her eyes with clean cotton wool dipped in cooled boiled water. Clean around her face and mouth.

4 Wash and rinse her hair, holding her head over the bath. Pat her head dry. Unwrap your baby, place one arm under her shoulders, and the other under her bottom, and lower her gently into the bath.

5 Supporting her neck and shoulders, wash and rinse her with your free hand. Slide your free arm under her bottom and lift her out gently. Wrap her in a towel and pat her dry. Keep your baby covered while you dress her and put on a clean nappy.

Warning

Never leave a young baby unattended in the bath even for a second. A baby can drown in less than an inch of water.

SLEEPING

Babies vary in the amount of time they sleep, but this is often less than parents expect. On average, new babies may be awake for six to eight hours in every 24 and usually sleep in naps of three to five hours.

CRYING

Crying is your baby's way of telling you she needs something. Gradually, you will learn to distinguish between different cries, such as hunger or tiredness. If your child will not stop crying or appears in pain, contact your doctor.

REDUCING THE RISK OF COT DEATH

Sudden infant death or cot death is rare, but research suggests there are ways in which you may be able to reduce the risk:

- Place your baby on the back to sleep, unless advised otherwise.
- Don't smoke during pregnancy or after the birth and do not expose your baby to tobacco smoke or smoky atmospheres.
- Don't let your baby get too hot. Use light layers of bedding.
- Contact your doctor if you think your baby is unwell.
- Don't let your baby sleep on a secondhand mattress or use a pillow.
- Don't let your baby's head get covered by bedclothes. Place her feet at the foot of the bed so that she cannot wriggle down.

5

FEEDING YOUR BABY

How you choose to feed your baby is a personal decision that only you can make. Breastfeeding offers many benefits for both mother and baby that formula milk is unable to duplicate. But for those who decide that they do not want to breastfeed, formula milk provides all the nutrients a baby needs.

BENEFITS OF BREAST MILK

■ Breast milk contains the correct proportions of nutrients needed for growth and development in the first few months of life. It's the right temperature, does not need sterilizing equipment, and is free and readily available.

■ Antibodies help to protect your baby against infections such as diarrhoea and vomiting; coughs and colds; urinary and ear infections.

■ Breast milk may reduce the risk of cot death, help to prevent juvenile diabetes and protect against allergies. Some studies have found that breastfed children have better dental health, fewer bowel problems and fewer speech problems than formula-fed babies.

■ Breastfeeding helps you develop a close bond with your baby, regain your figure more quickly and may reduce the risk of developing breast and ovarian cancer in later life.

BREASTFEEDING TIPS

■ At the beginning of a feed, your baby takes in low calorie "fore milk". As she continues feeding, this changes to high calorie "hindmilk". It is therefore important that your baby empties one breast before you offer her the other.

■ Let your baby feed on demand. Don't try to "build up" your supply by cutting out breastfeeding and offering formula instead. The more you feed, the more milk your breasts make.

■ The sucking action of a breastfed baby is different from that of a baby taking a bottle. When bottle feeding, the cheeks are sucked inwards; with breastfeeding, the jaw muscles work rhythmically, as far back as the ears. If your baby's cheeks cave in, she is not properly attached. Don't be discouraged if your baby takes a little time to learn to latch on properly. Remember, breastfeeding is a skill to be learned and practised.

■ If you are having difficulty, get help. The NCT and La Leche League (see p.111) have trained counsellors who can help you overcome breastfeeding problems.

HEALTH AND DIET WHEN BREASTFEEDING

You will need about 500 extra calories a day. Try to eat the balanced diet you followed during pregnancy and to include something from the four food groups daily. Three small meals are better than one large one, and have healthy snacks in-between meals. Don't force yourself to drink large quantities of fluid. Be guided by your body and drink when you feel thirsty.

5

BREASTFEEDING POSITIONS

Correct positioning at the breast is essential for successful breastfeeding. Otherwise, the baby will chew on your nipple, making you sore and frustrating her; it also means you will produce less milk. If she is properly positioned, she will have all of the nipple and most of the areola (the dark skin around your nipple) in her mouth.

1 Sit in a comfortable position, well supported with your baby supported in your arms, her head and shoulders facing your breast, and her nose on the same level as your nipple. Place the baby on a pillow to raise her up to the correct level if you have had a caesarean section to avoid putting stress on your scar.

2 If you are breastfeeding at night or if you find it difficult to sit because of painful stitches, you may feel more comfortable lying down. Lie down on your side with enough pillows to keep you propped up and place the baby on her side with her mouth in line with your breast.

SUCCESSFUL BOTTLEFEEDING

If you choose not to breastfeed, there is a wide choice of formula milk to choose from. To avoid infection, all equipment must be thoroughly cleaned and sterilized.

1 Wash bottles in hot soapy water, cleaning the inside with a baby brush. Rinse. Turn the teat inside out and clean the milky film. Rinse.

2 Sterilize the bottles, discs, rings, caps and teats by putting them into a sterilizing solution or a steam sterilizer for the recommended amount of time, or by stacking them in the dishwasher on the hottest temperature cycle.

3 Wash your hands and make sure you have everything ready. Make up the feed by boiling some fresh water and letting it cool. Measure the required amount of powder and add the formula to the correct amount of water.

4 Stir well and pour into individual bottles. Place the teats upside down in the bottles, add the sealing caps and shake well. Store in the refrigerator for up to 24 hours). To warm the milk, stand the bottle in a jug of hot water or an electric bottle warmer. **It is considered dangerous to heat a bottle of milk in a microwave because it will heat unevenly.** Check the temperature of the milk by dropping a little on the inside of your wrist. To feed your baby, hold her well propped up.

5

REMINDERS

The first few days and weeks with a newborn are exhausting, but infinitely rewarding. This checklist will remind you of the most important points to think about.

CARING FOR YOURSELF

- Expect the first few weeks to be hectic and haphazard and decide what your priorities are.
- Ask for pain relief if you need it.
- Get plenty of rest. Try to have a short rest while your baby is sleeping.
- Only do essential housework and limit your visitors.
- Don't feel guilty about taking time for yourself.
- Don't be a martyr. Accept any help that is offered, or if necessary, ask for it.
- If you feel you may be suffering from postnatal depression, ask for help.
- Do your pelvic floor exercises every day. Strong pelvic floor muscles help control your bladder after childbirth and are important in lovemaking.
- Watch your posture. Stand tall, stomach in, knees slightly bent.
- Always lift your baby or any other object with your knees bent.
- Change or attend to your baby on a surface that is the right height for you.
- Don't start dieting. Foods such as cereals, sandwiches, cheese, yoghurt and fruit are easy to prepare if you don't have time for cooked meals. Don't feel guilty about having take-away meals, but make sure they are as healthy as possible.
- Babies don't know what a routine is, and you will wear yourself out unnecessarily if you try to impose one.
- No parent is perfect: those who try to be feel guilty when they fail.

CARING FOR YOUR BABY

- Very few babies look perfect at birth and most irregularities will disappear within a few weeks.
- Many mothers and fathers do not fall in love or "bond" with their baby at first; a parent-child relationship grows and matures.
- When picking up your baby or when changing, bathing or feeding her, always hold her firmly, and talk to her softly and gently, making eye contact.
- Give young brothers or sisters extra cuddles and reassurance that you still love them. Involve them in helping with the baby as much as possible.
- Correct positioning at the breast is essential for successful breastfeeding. Ask for help (over the phone if necessary) if you need it.
- The more you feed your baby, the more milk you will produce.
- If you are bottlefeeding your baby, sterilize all your equipment.
- All babies settle eventually.

5

Your Personal File

Calling the doctor 102
Which symptoms require medical attention

In an emergency 103
What to do when there is no time to get to the hospital

Pregnancy record 104
Keep your own pregnancy diary

Pregnancy essentials 106
What to pack for the hospital, what you should leave behind

Baby essentials 108
What your baby needs as well as optional first buys

Telephone numbers 110
Write down important telephone numbers here

Useful addresses 111
Who to contact if you have any problems

YOUR PERSONAL FILE

Although every woman experiences her pregnancy in a way that is unique for her, there are also a number of factors that are common to every pregnancy. Most pregnant women also have many questions that need answers: what symptoms should I worry about? what do I need to see me through pregnancy and to take to hospital with me? what should I buy for my baby?

The following pages are intended to help you get organized and to plan ahead. This is also where important information can be kept in one place for you to find easily.

In this section you will find space to record important telephone numbers and addresses and a checklist of symptoms that make a call to your doctor wise. There is also room for you to record appointment dates for antenatal classes and test results; and a quick reference list of what to buy for you and your baby.

6

CALLING THE DOCTOR

The majority of women go through their pregnancy without any serious health problems, but occasionally problems arise that need advice or urgent attention from a doctor. Below is a list of signs and symptoms to help you recognize early when help may be required. Some symptoms such as a mild illness may just need general advice from your doctor or nurse-midwife. Others, such as vaginal bleeding with abdominal pain, severe abdominal pain, severe itching, high blood pressure or symptoms of pre-eclampsia are medical emergencies and you should contact a doctor or hospital immediately.

SYMPTOMS REQUIRING MEDICAL ATTENTION

- Vaginal bleeding, other than light spotting.
- Signs of pre-eclampsia including: high blood pressure, severe headache, dizziness, swelling of hands, face or feet, blurred vision, spots before your eyes or flashing lights, vomiting in late pregnancy, large and sudden weight gain or pain in upper abdomen.
- Symptoms of an infectious disease, such as a rash or fever.
- Contact with an infectious disease to which you are not immune, such as chicken pox or rubella (German measles).
- Severe generalised itching in the last three months of pregnancy. This may be a warning sign of *obstetric cholestatis*, a rare liver disorder. Other signs may include jaundice or yellow skin, pale stools and dark urine.
- Symptoms of a urinary tract infection including: frequent passing of urine with pain, burning or discomfort, low back pain, fever or chills and blood in the urine.
- Abdominal pain, especially if accompanied by vaginal bleeding. In the first three months of pregnancy, severe abdominal pain accompanied by bleeding may signal a miscarriage.
- Severe vomiting.
- Signs of labour including: breaking of your waters and contractions (see p. 72).
- A greenish discharge when your waters break needs urgent medical attention. Call an ambulance.
- Symptoms of any other infection or illness including:
    - Severe sore throat
    - High fever
    - Swollen glands
    - General fatigue or malaise with aching muscles or joint pains
- A general feeling that "something is wrong".

IN AN EMERGENCY

In the event of an emergency, there may be various people whom you or someone else will need to contact. Keep all the telephone numbers you might need in an emergency (see p.110) next to your telephone.

EMERGENCY DELIVERY IF YOU ARE ALONE

If you find that you are going into strong labour and do not have time to get to the hospital:

■ Try to stay calm. A fast labour means that your body and your baby are working well together.

■ Call the emergency service and tell them what's happening.

■ Try to find a neighbour or someone to help. Bang on a party wall, open the front door and shout if you can, phone anyone who lives close.

■ Start panting to prevent you from bearing down.

■ If you have time, wash your hands and vaginal area.

■ Find clean towels, a sheet or something to wrap the baby in.

■ Try to heat the room and spread some plastic sheeting, clean sheets, towels or newspapers on the floor, sofa or bed.

■ Lie down on these, either propped up on pillows or on your side, and await help.

■ If your baby arrives before help does, pant her out gently. Cradle her head while you wait for her body to emerge, but don't pull on her head. Check whether the umbilical cord is around her neck – it will feel like a thick rope. If it is, gently work it over her head. Don't tug on it.

■ Wrap your baby in whatever is available and wipe away any mucus from the nose. If necessary, clear her mouth with your finger.

■ If the cord is long enough, let your baby suck on your breast, even if you are not going to breastfeed.

■ Don't try to pull or push the placenta out. If it expels itself, wrap it up if possible and keep it at the same level as the baby.

■ Keep yourself and your baby warm under covers until help arrives.

BLEEDING IN PREGNANCY

■ Try to stay calm.

■ Call the doctor, ambulance or hospital, or ask someone to do this for you.

■ Go to bed or lie down until help arrives.

■ Keep any blood stained clothes; don't flush away any blood or clots until you have been seen by the doctor. Pinkish or greyish material may be pregnancy tissue and should be preserved so that the doctor can check if a miscarriage is complete.

■ Don't have anything to eat or drink until the doctor allows you to.

6

PREGNANCY RECORD

These pages can be used to keep your own pregnancy diary, including important dates such as test dates and your antenatal clinic and classes appointments. You can also record how you feel physically and emotionally.

PERSONAL INFORMATION

DATE OF MY LAST MENSTRUAL PERIOD   _____

DATE I FOUND OUT I WAS PREGNANT   _____

DATE MY BABY IS EXPECTED   _____

DATE I FIRST HEARD MY BABY'S HEARTBEAT   _____

DATE I FIRST FELT MY BABY MOVE   _____

DATE MY LABOUR BEGAN   _____

MY BIRTH COMPANION   _____

MY BABY WAS
BORN _____   TIME _____
WEIGHT _____   LENGTH _____

MY BLOOD TYPE _____   MY PREPREGANCY WEIGHT _____

MEDICATIONS	DOSE	DATE STARTED	DATE ENDED
Folic acid	400mg daily		

6

SPECIAL TESTS

Date	Type of procedure	Result

ANTENATAL APPOINTMENTS

Date & Time	Weeks	Blood pressure	Weight	Questions to ask/comments

ANTENATAL CLASSES

Name of tutor _____ Place _____
Date _____ Time _____
Special notes _____

DENTAL APPOINTMENTS

Date _____ Time _____
Date _____ Time _____

6

PREGNANCY ESSENTIALS

What clothes you buy during pregnancy will depend to a large extent on what you already have in your wardrobe, what you can adapt, and your financial budget. When buying new clothes, you also need to consider the use you will get afterwards, especially if you are going to breastfeed. In this case, the clothes should be front opening (see pp. 38–39 for pregnancy clothing essentials). You will also need to think about what you need to take to the hospital for you and your baby.

WHAT TO PACK FOR HOSPITAL

Many babies tend to arrive before they are due, so to be on the safe side have your bags packed by about 36 weeks. The hospital may give you a list of items to take in with you. If not, try to find out what the hospital provides and what you need to supply for yourself.

You may find it helpful to pack three bags – one for your hospital stay, one for labour and a going-home bag with clothes for you and your baby. You do not need to take all the items listed. Check you have packed the essential ones, and consider what others would be useful for you, depending on your proposed length of stay.

LABOUR BAG

- Sponge or facecloth for wiping your face. A natural sponge is softer than synthetic.
- Oil or lotion for your birth partner to massage you.
- Lip balm.
- Thick socks (for cold feet in labour).
- Snacks for your partner and yourself, if allowed (for example fruit, rice crackers, crispbread, fruit bars, cartons of fruit juice).
- Camera and film and/or camcorder.
- A large hand mirror if you want to see your baby being born (some hospitals have mirrors, so check).
- Ties or clips for long hair.
- Maternity sanitary pads.
- Waterspray or eau de cologne to cool your face.
- Hot-water bottle for use between contractions.
- Cassette player and tapes.
- Nightdress or old T-shirt, if you don't want to wear a hospital gown.

FOR YOUR HOSPITAL STAY

- 1–3 nightdresses, depending on the length of your stay; these should be front opening if you are going to breastfeed.
- Light dressing gown and slippers.
- Two or three nursing/ordinary bras.
- Comfortable cotton panties.
- Packet of maternity sanitary towels.
- Washbag containing soap, facecloths, toothbrush, toothpaste, mouthwash, shampoo, deodorant, hairbrush and comb and make up if used.
- Washbag for birth partner with similar items.
- 1–2 small towels for face and hands/1 large for shower.
- Wet wipes – useful for a quick wipe of your hands or face.
- Box of tissues.
- Moisturizing cream/body lotion.
- Talcum powder.
- Coins and phonecard for telephone (you probably won't be able to use a mobile phone; they interfere with hospital equipment).
- Address or telephone book with essential numbers.
- Books, magazines, pen, stationery, stamps, birth announcement cards, games, knitting.

GOING-HOME BAG

Your partner could bring this in later if necessary.
- Loose comfortable clothes, such as skirt, trousers, sweater or dress.
- Underwear, including tights if necessary.
- Shoes or sandals if you have none in hospital.
- Coat or jacket if cold.
- Money for taxi if necessary.

FOR THE BABY
- Vest.
- 1–2 nappies.
- Stretchsuit.
- Cardigan.
- Hat.
- Shawl or blanket.

- If you are going home by car, use an approved car seat or carrycot with a fitted restraint to carry your baby. Some hospitals will hire these. It is not safe to carry your baby in your arms.
- Check what items the hospital will provide and what you need to supply: napkins, towels, baby clothes, sheets, cotton wool or any other items, and pack these as necessary in your hospital bag.

6

BABY ESSENTIALS

The list of "essentials" for your baby can seem endless, and the choice of baby goods bewildering. But although it is natural for parents to feel they want to give their baby the best of everything, you don't need to break the bank. After the baby's basic needs for love, warmth and nourishment, material needs are few. If money is tight, remember, your baby is not going to know whether she is bathed in a plastic bowl, the kitchen sink or in an expensive babybath with a stand. Or realize whether she is dressed in a designer label or secondhand chainstore stretchsuit. Some larger items can also be bought later or secondhand, or you may be able to borrow from friends and relatives.

GENERAL TIPS

■ Decide on your priorities: make a list of essential buys that you will need as soon as your baby is born, a second list of what you can buy later, and a third list of luxury or optional buys.

■ If you are in doubt about buying something, wait until after the birth to see if you really need it.

■ Check with friends and relatives for items to borrow, and secondhand shops and markets for bargains.

■ Collect as many store or mail-order catalogues as you can. Look through these to see what's available and compare prices. Accept trial offers of nappies and toiletries.

■ Don't buy too many "first size" clothes – babies soon grow out of them.

■ Think about how much space you have available at home before buying a large item such as a pram.

BEDTIME NEEDS

■ Moses basket/portable crib or carrycot/cot. Check, if buying secondhand, that these conform to government safety standards. A Moses basket should not be placed directly on the floor, so you may need a stand, too.

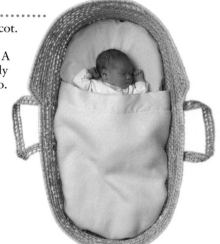

■ New mattress to fit the above, and conforming to government safety standards (Recent research has found that secondhand mattresses could be a factor in some cot deaths.)

■ 4–6 flame-retardant crib sheets

■ 4–6 cotton crib/cot blankets

■ 2 light crib/cot covers.

BABY'S FIRST ESSENTIALS

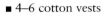

- 4–6 cotton vests
  - 4–6 stretch suits or 4–6 long nightdresses (low flammability)
  - 2–3 cardigans/matineé jackets
  - 3–4 pairs socks or booties
  - 1–2 woolly hats or summer bonnets. (If these won't stay on, wrap your baby's head in the blanket or shawl.)
    - 2 pairs mittens
    - 4–6 bibs
  - Shawl or carrying blanket for outdoors
- Weekly supply of newborn-size disposable nappies or 24 cloth nappies and protective pants.

OTHER NEEDS

- 6 bottles, teats, sterilizing equipment (a plastic covered container can serve as a chemical sterilizing unit), and formula milk if you are not breastfeeding.
- First car seat if you have a car.
- Toiletries such as cotton balls, mild soap or baby wash lotion.
- Soft towel for bathing.

OPTIONAL FIRST BUYS

- Pram/pushchair/buggy
- Sling
- Baby bath
- Changing mat and changing bag
- Baby monitor.

SAFETY FIRST

- Make sure any new or secondhand equipment conforms to government safety regulations, where applicable.
- A baby does not need a pillow under the age of one.
- Make sure the mattress fits the crib/cot/basket; don't buy secondhand.
- Duvets are not recommended for babies under the age of one, since they can overheat the baby.
- If you buy a baby nest, only use it for carrying. Don't let your baby sleep in one indoors – they can overheat your baby and be dangerous.

6

TELEPHONE NUMBERS

MY PARTNER CAN BE REACHED AT _____

EMERGENCY SERVICES   Tel. No: _____

FAMILY DOCTOR
Name: _____ Tel. No: _____
Address: _____

OBSTETRICIAN
Name: _____ Tel. No: _____
Address: _____

NURSE-MIDWIFE
Name: _____ Tel. No: _____
Address: _____

HOSPITAL
Name: _____ Tel. No: _____
Address: _____

NEXT OF KIN
Name: _____ Tel. No: _____
Address: _____

NEIGHBOUR
Name: _____ Tel. No: _____

NEIGHBOUR
Name: _____ Tel. No: _____

CHILDMINDER/NURSERY/SCHOOL
Name: _____ Tel. No: _____
Address _____

HEALTH INSURANCE COMPANY
Name: _____ Tel. No: _____
Address: _____
Policy no: _____

6

USEFUL ADDRESSES

GENERAL SUPPORT OR ADVICE DURING AND/OR AFTER PREGNANCY

Association for Postnatal Illness 25 Jerdan Place, London SW6 1BE

CRY-SIS (Babies with crying/sleep problems) BM CRY-SIS, London WCIN 3XX

Family Planning Association 2–12 Pentoville Road, London N1 9FP

Genetic Interest Group 29–35 Farringdon Road, London EC1M 3JB

Health Link Wales/Cadwyn Iach Cymru Ffynnon-las Ty Glas Avenue, Llanishen, Cardiff CF4 5DZ

Maternity Alliance (maternity rights) 45 Beech Street, London EC2P 2LX

MAMA (Meet-A-Mum Association) 26 Avenue Road, London SE25

National Council for One-Parent Families 255 Kentish Town Rd, London NW5 2LX

NCT (National Childbirth Trust – also for breastfeeding) Alexandra House, Oldham Terrace, London W3 6NH

Twins and Multiple Births Association PO Box 30, Little Sutton, South Wirral, L66 1TH

BREASTFEEDING

Association of Breastfeeding Mothers 26 Holmshaw Close, London SE26 4TG

La Leche League (Great Britain) BM 3424, London WC1N 3XX

MOTHERS OR BABIES WITH SPECIAL NEEDS

BLISS (Baby Life Support Systems – also for postnatal depression) 17–21 Emerald St, London WC1N 2QL

British Diabetic Association 10 Queen Anne Street, London W1M OBD **and** John Gibson House, 257 Lisburn Road, Belfast BT9 7EN

British Epilepsy Association Anstey House, 40 Hanover Square, Leeds LSE 1BE

Contact a Family (Support groups for all disabilities) 170 Tottenham Court Road, London W1P OHA

Disabled Living Foundation 380 Harrow Road, London W9 2HU

Down's Syndrome Association 155 Micham Road, London SW17 9PG

National Asthma Campaign Providence House, Providence Place, London N1 0NT

Sickle Cell Society 54 Station Road, London NW10 4UA

WHEN A BABY DIES

Compassionate Friends 53 North Street, Bristol BS3 1EN

Foundation for the Study of Infant Deaths 14 Halkin Street, London SW1X 7DP

Miscarriage Association Clayton Hospital, Northgate, Wakefield, West Yorkshire WF1 3JS

SAFTA (Support after Termination for Abnormality) 73 Charlotte Street, London W1P 1LB

Scottish Cot Death Trust Royal Hospital for Sick Children, Yorkhill, Glasgow G3 8SJ

Stillbirth and Neonatal Death Society 28 Portland Place, London W1N 4DE

6

ACKNOWLEDGMENTS

t = top, b = bottom, l = left, r = right, c = centre

Picture credits
5 The Stock Market; 6t Andrew Sydenham; 6b Andrew Sydenham,
Laura Wickenden; 6br Andrew Sydenham; 12 Laura Wickenden;
14 Jacqui Farroi/Bubbles; 15 Laura Wickenden; 16 Jo Foord; 17 Holy
Name Hospital, New Jersey; 19 Angela Hampton/Bubbles;21 Laura
Wickenden; 24t Laura Wickenden; 24b Jo Foord; 26t Andrew
Sydenham; 26b Jennie Woodcock/Bubbles; 29 Christine Hanscomb, Jo
Foord, Andrew Sydenham, Laura Wickenden; 31 Laura Wickenden;
32 Andrew Sydenham; 33 Andrew Sydenham; 34–35t Andrew
Sydenham; 35b Loisjoy Thurston/Bubbles; 38 Laura Wickenden;
39t Andrew Sydenham; 39b Laura Wickenden; 40 Laura Wickenden;
41 Andrew Sydenham; 43 Matthew Ward; 44 Jeff Hunter/The Image
Bank; 45 Matthew Ward; 48–49 Laura Wickenden; 50–51 Laura
Wickenden; 52t Andrew Sydenham; 52b Laura Wickenden; 53 Laura
Wickenden; 54l Iain Bagwell; 54r Laura Wickenden; 55 Laura
Wickenden; 56–57 Andrew Sydenham; 58–59 Laura Wickenden;
61 Laura Wickenden; 63 Jo Foord; 65 The Stock Market; 68 The
Stock Market; 68 inset The Stock Market; 73 Laura Wickenden;
75 Laura Wickenden; 78 Laura Wickenden; 79t Jo Foord; 79c Jo
Foord; 79b Laura Wickenden; 82 Frans Rombout/Bubbles; 85 Andrew
Sydenham; 87 Andrew Sydenham; 89 Andrew Sydenham; 90 Laura
Wickenden; 91 Frans Rombout/Bubbles; 92 Andrew Sydenham;
93 Loisjoy Thurston/Bubbles; 94 Andrew Sydenham, Laura
Wickenden; 95 Andrew Sydenham; 96 Andrew Sydenham; 99 Andrew
Sydenham; 101 Andrew Sydenham; 104 Andrew Sydenham;
106 Laura Wickenden; 107 Andrew Sydenham; 108 The Stock
Market; 109t Laura Wickenden; 109b Andrew Sydenham

Illustration credits
13 Kevin Jones; 72 and 80 Michael Courtney; 77 and 81 Mick
Saunders; 66 and 67 Chris Forsey